The MANCHESTER Cook Book

A celebration of the amazing food & drink on our doorstep.
Featuring over 55 stunning recipes.

The Manchester Cook Book

©2015 Meze Publishing. All rights reserved.

First edition printed in 2015 in the UK.

ISBN: 978-1-910863-01-5

Thank you: Aiden Byrne, Simon Rogan, Simon Wood & Hospitality Action

Compiled by: Anna Tebble

Written by: Kate Eddison

Photography by:
Marc Barker (www.marcabarker.com)

Tim Green (www.timgreenphotographer.co.uk)

Additional Photography:
www.jamesbrownphotographer.co.uk

www.bacononthebeech.com

Edited by: Rachel Heward, Phil Turner

Designed by: Paul Cocker, Marc Barker, Phil Turner

Cover art: Luke Prest, www.lukeprest.com

Contributors: Kelsie Marsden, Faye Bailey, Sarah Koriba, Kerre Chen, Emily Beaumont

Published by Meze Publishing Limited
Unit 1 Beehive Works
Milton Street
Sheffield S3 7WL
Web: www.mezepublishing.co.uk
Tel: 0114 275 7709
Email: info@mezepublishing.co.uk

FOREWORD

"The vibe in Manchester is electric ... and the number of restaurants opening is proof of this." – Aiden Byrne, Manchester House.

Since opening in 2013, Manchester has been very kind to us.

We have filled our restaurant pretty much each lunch and dinner since opening and that is credit to Manchester's desire for a bloody good plate of food.

I see us as being very lucky because Manchester is going through a mini boom at the moment and I believe we have opened just at the right time. In the past, there have been numerous restaurateurs that have come to the city and tried to dictate to Mancunians how they should dine out, but since being here, we have discovered that people just want to enjoy themselves and demand the best hospitality... and rightly so.

Not wanting to repeat myself, but what I love about Manchester is the fact that our diners want to have fun and feel relaxed and this is the exact vibe you get when you come to Manchester House. We of course work hard to be as professional as possible and deliver the best product and service that we can, but we do it with a smile on our faces.

The vibe in and around Manchester is electric, the sense of positivity is contagious and the number of restaurants that are opening is proof of this.

Manchester is surrounded by countryside on all sides, therefore our larder is very extensive. We don't have to look very far for the best ingredients, and inevitably as the demand rises the supply will follow.

The broad spectrum of food offerings is overwhelming, with British, Thai, Moroccan, French, Lebanese, steak houses, Pan Asian and burger joints, and not forgetting the whole of Rusholme's Curry Mile, which serves up some of the best Indian food in the UK.

Aiden Byrne

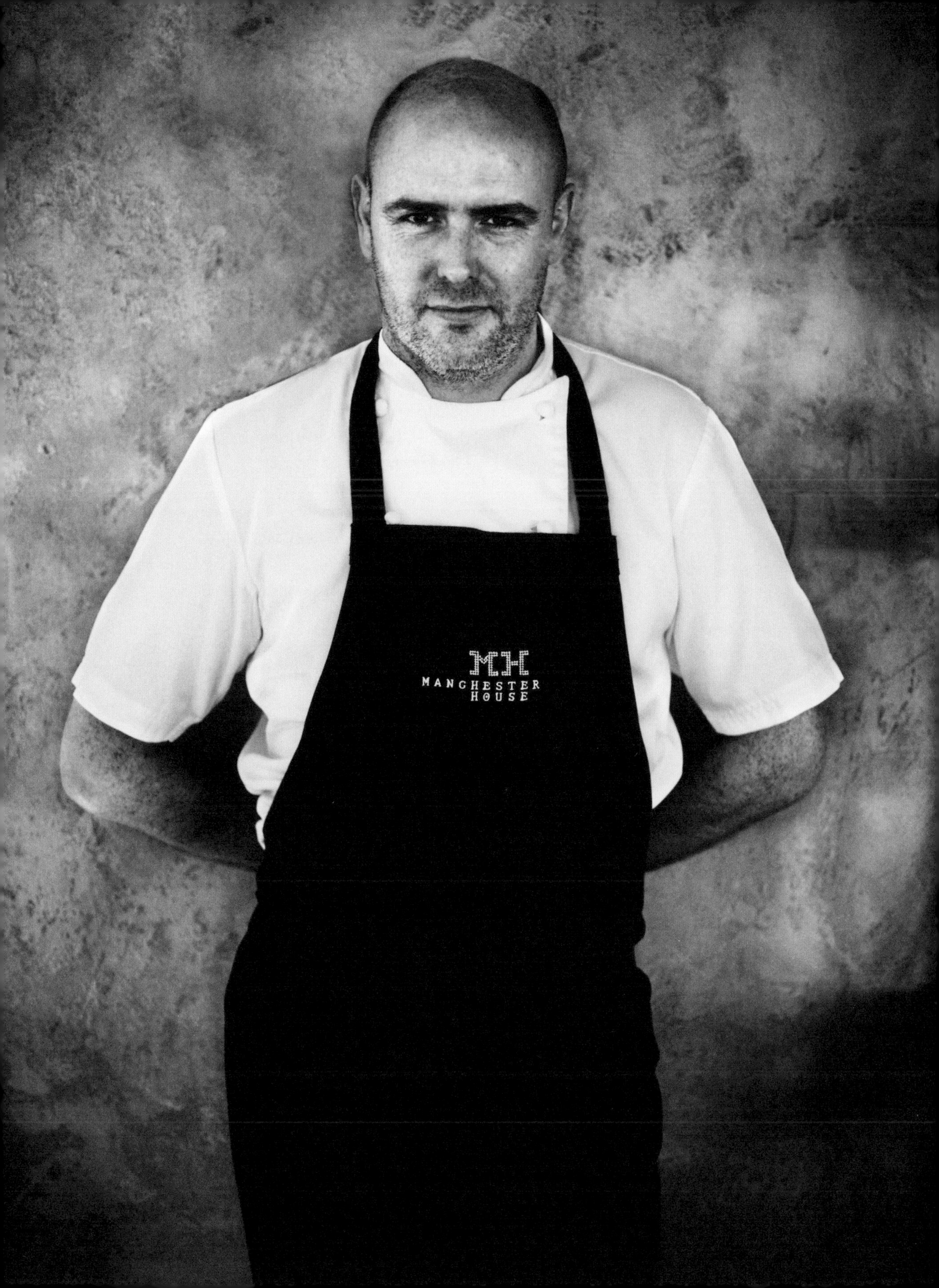
MH
MANCHESTER
HOUSE

CONTENTS

Editorial

Credits	4
Foreword by Aiden Byrne	8
My food memories by Anna Tebble	12
Kate Eddison's Manchester	12
Hospitality Action	16
The directory	210

Guest recipes

Simon Wood – Ballotine of Chicken	167

Chef recipes

63 Degrees

From Paris to Manchester	20
Croustillant d'escargots, espuma persillé	23

Abel Heywood

Not Your Ordinary Pub	24
Abel Heywood Braised Short rib of Beef	27
Abel Heywood Seabass, Cockles and Mussels	29
Abel Heywood Eggs Atlantic	31

Albert's

Albert's Story	32
Albert's Chilli Prawn Linguini	35
Albert's Choo Chee Seafood Curry	37
Albert's Chocolate Volcano	39

Ancoats Coffee Company

Spilling The Beans	40
How To Use An Aeropress	43

Bisous Bisous

Pastries From Paris	44
Bisous Bisous Gateau Opera	47

Bollywood Masala

Taking The Starring Role	48

Brassica Grill

Understated Excellence	50
Brassica Grill Roast Rump of High Peak Lamb	53

The Bury Black Pudding Company

The Only Bury Black Pudding on the Block	54
Lamb Hot Pot with Black Pudding	59

The Butchers Quarter

From the Farm to the City	60
Butcher's Quarter Venison Steak	63

Croma

A Pizza the Action	64
Croma Aglefino Pizza	67
Croma Funghi Di Bosco	69
Croma Martini	71

Dish Ran away with the Spoon

Tea Time Treats	72
Dish Ran Away Strawberry Eton Mess Cake	77

Dormouse Chocolate

Bean to Bar Chocolate	78
Dormouse Simple Chocolate Truffles	78

Epicerie Ludo

Bienvenue à Chorlton	80
Epicerie Ludo Tarte Flambee	83
Epicerie Ludo Baie Chocolat Passion	85

The George Charles

By George	86
George Charles Chocolate Orange Fondant	89

Harvey Nichols Manchester Second Floor Bar and Brasserie

    Bold as Brass   90

    Second Floor Bar and Brasserie Tandoori Monkfish   93

    Second Floor Bar and Brasserie Assiette of Honey   95

    Second Floor Bar Garden of Eden   97

    Second Floor Bar Conquistador   97

Iberica

    A Taste of Spain in Spinningfields   98

    Iberica Twice-Cooked Lamb   101

Lime

    The Heart and Soul of Salford Quays   102

    Lime Roast Hake with Chickpeas and Chorizo   105

MAD

    We are Totally Mad for it   106

    Rosylee Bubble and Squeak   109

    The Fitzgerald French Martinilla   109

    Infamous Diner Corn Dogs   111

    Infamous Diner Buttermilk Pancakes   113

    Walrus BBQ Chicken Wings   115

    Walrus Solero   115

The Manchester Tart Company

    Award Winning Pies & Tarts   116

Manchester House

    Another Level   120

    Manchester House Hay-Baked Mallard   123

The Metropolitan

    Meet and Eat at The Met   124

    The Metropolitan Sea Bass with Chickpea   127

Mish Mash

    All Set to Mix Things Up   129

    Mish Mash Mojito Chicken   131

Mr Cooper's House & Garden

    Stay True to Your Roots   132

    Mr Cooper's Sage-Crusted Pork Chop   135

Palate

    Palate Pleasers   136

    Palate Hot Coronation Chicken   139

The Parlour

    The Spirit of Chorlton   140

    The Parlour Cheshire Ox Cheek   145

Podium Restaurant

    A Step Above   146

    Truffle Pasta and Wild Mushroom Open Lasagne   149

Pokusevski's

    Delis with a Difference   150

    Pokusevski's Chefs Breakfast   153

    Pokusevski's Courgette and Lemon Cake   155

The Rose Garden

    Burton Rose   156

    The Rose Garden Parma Ham-Wrapped Monkfish   159

    The Rose Garden Rhubarb and Ginger   161

Salvi's

    Little Italy   162

    Salvi's Polpo Alla Luciana   165

Slice Pizza & Bread Bar

    A Slice of Rome   168

    Slice Mozzarella, Broccoli, Sausage and Chilli Pizza   171

Tampopo

    The Perfect Bowl Of Noodles   172

    Tampopo Thai Mussels Tom Yam Style   175

    Tampopo Vegetable Tempura   177

    Tampopo Thai Basil in a Fiery Oyster Sauce   179

Teacup Kitchen

    Time for Tea   180

    Teacup Kitchen Exoticado   183

    Teacup Kitchen Flourless Chocolate Cake   185

Trove

    Treasure Trove   186

    Trove White Sourdough   189

The Victorian Chop House Company

    The Best of British   190

    The Albert Sq Chop House Seared Scallops   193

    Mr Thomas Famous Corned Beef House   195

    Sam's Rice Pudding   197

The White Hart

    Fine Dining with Rustic Charm   198

    The White Hart Rhubarb Soufflé   201

Zouk Tea Bar and Grill

    More Than a Curry   204

    Zouk Tea Bar Chicken Haleem   207

Zymurgorium

    The Science of Brewing   208

    Zymurgorium Strataspheric Aviator   211

    Zymurgorium Cranachan   211

Exploring MANCHESTER

Meze Publishing's Anna Tebble talks about her food journey
and discovering the secrets of Manchester.

My first vivid food memory is a family friend looking after me whilst I was poorly and off school around the age of 6. I distinctly remember her baking whilst I was at her house and it prompted an amazing feeling of comfort.

I have definitely inherited my Nanna's food memory; she could always remember a day out, no matter how long ago it was, by what she had to eat that day. As a child, my family were more about picnics rather than eating out at restaurants. This, coupled with my Mum being a fantastic cook, has undeniably influenced my love for home-cooking. I love nothing better than spending a whole day leisurely preparing a special meal with a glass of wine and a good playlist for company.

My social life is unashamedly centred around food. When I look at my closest friends, it is as if I hand-picked them solely based on their dedication to food. My friends are undeniably my inspiration to experiment with new ingredients and, when I'm not cooking, I can be found mulling over my next culinary project.

I have been lucky enough to travel extensively, which has broadened my culinary horizons. It would be fair to say many of the destinations have been chosen purely on their food offerings, leading me to drag my other half on street food tours in Vietnam and make a beeline to the nearest food festival whilst in Scandinavia.

As a dedicated foodie, being able to compile a cook book in a city that is close to my heart has been an absolute delight. I lived in Manchester more years ago than I would like to admit and seeing the change in the foodie scene has been fascinating. I have relished having the opportunity to explore the food scene in Manchester and get a real feel for the close-knit foodie community that exists in this vast city.

I hope you get as much pleasure from perusing this book as I did compiling it.

Anna Tebble

My sister Nicola and I

Just a
NORTHERN LASS

Cook book author Kate Eddison is a northern girl at heart ... and the Manchester food scene more than satisfies her hunger pangs.

I've worked in food and drink publishing for eight happy years, and for me, there couldn't be a better job in the world. Surrounding yourself with people who are as obsessed with cooking as you are inspires creativity, passion and, let's face it, lots of yummy dinner ideas.

Having lived in London for the last eight years, it was, I hate to admit, with a little trepidation that I decided to make the move to Manchester. I'm a northern girl and the north was pulling me home with its promises of vibrant cities, friendly folk and my mum's Sunday dinners, but I'd been a Londoner for so long – would I miss the myriad burger options, street food stalls and hipster watering holes in which I'd whiled away my twenties? Of course not.

Manchester is quite simply incredible. From the buzz of the Northern Quarter to the glamour of Spinningfields, the city centre is peppered with hidden bars, trendy pop-ups and world-class restaurants serving up truly amazing food. And it doesn't end in the city centre when vibrant communities such as Chorlton, Prestwich and Heaton Moor are bursting at the seams with independent shops, delis, pubs, restaurants and markets. I've spent the last three months eating my way around this city (all in the name of research, of course) and I've barely scratched the surface.

I've bought pigs' cheeks from The Butcher's Quarter and cooked up a storm, I've eaten pizza al taglio from Slice and felt like I'd been instantly transported to Rome, I've sauntered around Didsbury and sampled the plethora of pubs showcasing local food and beers. Yet despite my solid effort and expanding waistline, my list of 'places to try' is getting longer rather than shorter, because around every corner there is something new popping up or another Manchester institution that I realise I haven't yet tried.

Without doubt, the best thing about getting to write this book has been getting to know all the truly inspirational people who make up the gastronomic map of Manchester. There is a network of food-lovers who work together to weave a delicious tapestry of regional cuisine by supporting each other every single day. I'm talking about the delis who stock produce from independent makers, the restaurants who buy their meat from the local butcher, the butcher who sources his produce from the local farmer and the pubs who serve beer from Manchester breweries.

This is a city with so much to shout about. From culinary legends Aiden Byrne and Simon Rogan to independent producers hand-making award-winning products in their own kitchens, this is a city that lives and breathes all things food.

I hope you enjoy reading about these amazing people and places as much as I enjoyed getting to know them. Get stuck in. Read about it, go out and taste it, and then put your apron on and cook it.

Kate Eddison

Hospitality ACTION

Hospitality Action is the trade charity offering a crucial lifeline to people of all ages, working and retired, from the hospitality industry.

Whether they are approached by a chef, housekeeper, school cook or waiter, Hospitality Action will endeavour to support, whatever the difficulty.

Sometimes all it takes is a very small change in circumstances to tip the balance and turn a manageable situation into an unmanageable one. An extended illness, such as cancer, can lead to a sudden and unexpected drop in pay, whilst a relationship breakdown, bereavement or redundancy, can also put a strain on the household budget.

The charity strives to keep their support relevant to the industry and helps financially when required. Those at the start of their career are educated on the dangers of alcohol and drug misuse via a series of popular seminars. Those currently working can receive support via the Hospitality Action Employee Assistance Programme, 24 hours a day, 365 days per year, whilst industry retirees are welcome to join their very popular befriending scheme to help prevent loneliness and isolation.

The charity recently launched a brand new hard-hitting advertising campaign. The adverts feature images of five of the UK's most renowned chefs having fallen on hard times and aims to raise awareness of the charity and of the issues that can affect hospitality workers both past and present.

The UK-wide campaign depicts Hospitality Action Patron and Trustee Jason Atherton struggling with an addiction, Angela Hartnett illustrated as a victim of domestic violence, Tom Kerridge portrayed as someone suffering from a critical illness, Heston Blumenthal Principal Patron of Hospitality Action portrayed as suffering a serious injury and Ashley Palmer-Watts shown as a sufferer of depression.

The campaign will act as a startling reminder that these things can happen to anyone. Emma Astwood and Edna Bradshaw are just two people who have been helped by Hospitality Action, and we take a look at their stories here.

Domestic violence

Depression

Critical illness

Addiction

Emma Astwood, Housekeeper

Emma and her son moved to the north leaving a troubled past behind them. Happy in her job as a housekeeper Emma was devastated when she was diagnosed with breast cancer. Needing both chemotherapy and radiotherapy. She was forced to leave work and face the uncertain future. Struggling to come to terms with her diagnosis Emma worried she was becoming a burden on her family. Her many hospital visits added to her financial outgoings and her utility bills increased as she became more heat sensitive as a consequence of her treatment. No longer able to afford the rental on her washer/dryer Emma turned to Hospitality Action. We helped to buy a replacement enabling Emma to focus on her son, on her health and to become a little more self-reliant.

Edna Bradshaw, Barmaid

Edna worked as a barmaid for over a decade. Now in her seventies Edna suffers from painful chronic osteoporosis of the hip and spine. Her husband John has been diagnosed with prostate cancer and has sadly also undergone surgery for bowel cancer. Both Edna and John have mobility problems and really feel the cold, but with no savings to call upon, the couple found themselves unable to install central heating in their home. They relied only on a gas fire in the living room and their cooker for warmth. Edna and John contacted Hospitality Action and we were able to provide the couple with a grant towards the cost of installing a gas boiler and radiators so helping to keep them warm over the winter. John said: "The central heating has made a tremendous difference to our lives".

Hospitality Action receives no government funding and so is dependent on individuals and corporate bodies from within the hospitality industry to support its vital work.

If you would like to make a donation to Hospitality Action simply text Chef16 £5 to 70070

For more information and ways to support please contact:
Dawn Holding via dawn@dawnholding.co.uk
Visit: www.hospitalityaction.org.uk
Twitter: @HospActionNorth
Facebook: HospitalityAction
Registered Charity No: 1101083

Serious injury

From Paris to MANCHESTER

Classic French cooking has been brought to the Northern Quarter by the Moreau family, for whom precision and perfection are the keys to success at the aptly named 63 Degrees.

Nestled among the plethora of fashionable Northern Quarter eateries, this French restaurant, which opened in 2011, has quickly become a favourite among those looking for something a little bit special and a taste of classic French cooking.

Managed by Alex Moreau, with Alex's father Eric heading up the kitchen, this is a British-French family affair that takes the very best of French culinary heritage and adds some Manchester charm into the mix.

Every chef in the kitchen is French, and their skills and training are put to use in creating the impressive menu. The feel is classic French cooking with a modern approach. No more than three or four flavours feature in any dish, allowing the choice ingredients to take centre stage. Alex explains that in their pursuit of using the very best ingredients, they use a mixture of French and British suppliers, depending on the product.

For the cheeses, they use the finest French suppliers, and you would hardly expect any less. They also turn to our French neighbours to source the finest snails, chicken and pigeon, insisting on finding the perfect varieties for their dishes. However, when it comes to vegetables and salad, they prefer to use suppliers as local as possible to guarantee the freshest organic produce. For the rack of lamb with apricots, only the very best Welsh lamb is good enough for the discerning chef and the luxurious beef fillet is sourced from local legend W. H. Frost Butchers in Chorlton.

When so much effort goes into sourcing the perfect ingredients, it goes without saying that everything is hand-made each and every day at 63 Degrees. You won't find a freezer on the premises here. From the stock for the lobster risotto to the port reduction for the pigeon Rossini, every single element is prepared from scratch.

Fine wines, elegant Champagnes and luxurious cocktails complement the food, and in the light and modern surroundings, you can truly experience a perfect taste of Paris before returning to the bustling streets of the Northern Quarter.

63 Degrees
CROUSTILLANT D'ESCARGOTS, ESPUMA PERSILLÉ

Snails in a tuille basket, parsley foam.

We recommend this classic French dish to be served with a Chablis. Serves 4.

Ingredients

8 sheets feuilles de brick

3 ratte potatoes, sliced

24 Bourgogne snails, medium size

50g smoked bacon, cut into pieces

100g shiitake mushrooms, sliced

3 tbsp olive oil

Salt and pepper

For the garlic butter:

50g butter, at room temperature

6 cloves garlic, peeled and sliced

30g parsley, chopped

Salt and pepper

For the parsley foam:

200g cream

6 cloves garlic, peeled

100g parsley

Salt and pepper

Equipment:

4 aluminium circles (6cm diameter, 5cm height)

A cream whipper

2 gas cartridges

Chinois

Method

For the garlic butter, mix the butter, garlic, parsley, salt and pepper to a smooth mixture.

For the parsley foam, add the cream and garlic cloves to a saucepan, bring to boiling point, add the parsley and simmer for 2 minutes. Add salt and pepper and strain through a chinois. Leave to cool then pour into the cream whipper and set aside.

Preheat the oven to 180°C. Take the feuilles de brick, cut eight circles 16cm in diameter from the pastry and place two into each aluminium circle overlapping half of one circle on top of the other, then push gently down into circles to give them a tulip shape. Place in the preheated oven for 5 minutes. Remove from the mould and place on plates.

Fry the ratte potato slices in the olive oil until golden. Add the snails, bacon and shiitake mushrooms and cook for 5 minutes. Then add the garlic butter, cook until melted and season to taste.

Divide the mixture into four portions and place into each basket. Add the parsley foam on top and serve immediately.

Not Your ORDINARY PUB

Boutique hotel rooms set above a stunning and bustling pub and cosy restaurant – Abel Heywood in the Northern Quarter has got the whole night covered.

Located within the bustling Northern Quarter, Abel Heywood dares to be just that little bit different from its neighbours – mixing old-world charm and modern trends with relaxing vibes and an effortlessly warm welcome.

From entering the doors downstairs, the traditional pub greets you with everything you expect from a friendly local. It's the type of pub you can spend an entire Sunday in armed with a newspaper, while also being somewhere you can indulge in contemporary cocktails on a Friday night or simply enjoy a few post-work beers supplied by the famous Hydes brewery and Beer Studio. Comforting dishes feature on the regularly changing pub menu, from time-honoured classics to creative modern dishes.

Upstairs the menu changes along with the atmosphere. The cosy dining rooms are the ideal setting for a leisurely meal with some fine wines to choose from too. Head Chef Jamie Dargie changes his menu every six weeks to keep up to date with seasonal ingredients, but you can rely on the freshest meat, fish and desserts all sourced from the region and all home-cooked on site.

Upstairs again and the 15 boutique hotel rooms have been designed to balance modern luxury with stylish charm, whether it's a short stay in a city double or a special weekend in a loft room or suite. With a string of accolades under their belt already – named as one of the top ten pubs in the UK by Shortlist magazine and one of the top 100 best hotels by The Sunday Times for 2015 – it's no surprise that this beautiful boutique hotel is consistently in TripAdvisor's top rankings.

One thing you might wonder – just who was Abel Heywood? Dig a little into the history of this famous Mancunian and you'll uncover his fascinating rise from a poor background to establishing a working man's newspaper, "The Poor Man's Guardian", which led him into conflict with the law for his free press principles. Luckily, the hosts have produced some information on this Manchester hero, which makes the perfect morning reading over a lazy breakfast. They really have thought of everything.

Abel Heywood

BRAISED SHORT RIB OF BEEF

and matchstick chips.

This warming dish is popular when it appears on our pub menu. Ask your butcher for beef short ribs or 'Jacob's ladder'. The dehydrated tomatoes make a great snack with olives, if you decide to make a few extra! Serves 2.

Ingredients

1kg short rib of beef (Jacob's ladder)

300ml beef stock

250ml red wine

50g thyme

250g spinach

1 onion, sliced

2 Maris Piper potatoes

75g pancetta, diced

Olive oil

Salt and pepper

For the dehydrated tomatoes:

3 cherry tomatoes, halved

Smoked sea salt

Extra virgin olive oil

A little fresh thyme

For the shallots:

2 banana shallots

Olive oil

A little red wine

A little fresh thyme

1 clove garlic

Method

For the dehydrated tomatoes, preheat the oven to 90°C. Place the halved cherry tomatoes on a baking tray, season with smoked sea salt, extra virgin olive oil and fresh thyme. Cook in the preheated oven until they are dehydrated. Place in a bowl with the cooking juices and marinate in olive oil. Cover and store in the fridge.

For the shallots, preheat the oven to 180°C. Wrap the shallots in foil, adding a little olive oil, red wine, thyme and garlic before wrapping. Cook in the oven at 180°C for 20 minutes (you can do this in advance, if you like).

For the beef, preheat the oven to 170°C. Seal the beef in a heavy ovenproof pan until it is browned all over. Add the beef stock, red wine and thyme, cover and braise in the oven for 4 hours.

For the spinach purée, add the spinach to a pan of boiling water for 5 seconds, then transfer to a food processor and purée. Season to taste.

For the onion purée, fry the sliced onion in a frying pan with a little olive oil until they are a deep golden colour, then blend them to a purée and pass through a fine sieve.

Slice the potatoes into thin matchsticks and place in cold water.

When ready to serve, remove the beef from the cooking liquor and reduce the liquor down into a sauce. Reheat the beef in the reduced sauce. Drain and dry the chips, then deep-fry them until cooked and season. Pan-fry the pancetta. Gently heat both purées and use a palette knife to spread them onto the plates. Place the beef and shallot on top, add the pancetta and serve with the chips, sauce and tomatoes.

Abel Heywood
SEABASS, COCKLES AND MUSSELS

with samphire and tomato.

This light and fresh seafood dish is taken from our restaurant menu, which changes depending on seasonal produce available. Serves 2.

Ingredients

2 fillets of seabass, pin-boned

6 cockles

6 mussels

175g samphire

2 tomatoes

300ml fish stock

75ml white wine

100g butter

½ lemon

Method

Score the skin of the seabass fillets. Clean the mussels and wash the cockles under cold running water for 30 minutes until all the sand is removed. Discard any that are open and do not close when tapped against the work surface.

Blanch the samphire in boiling water and then place in iced water to retain its colour.

Remove the core from the tomatoes and cut a cross on the bottom. Place the tomatoes in boiling water for 30 seconds, then remove and add to iced water. Remove the skin – it should peel away easily. Remove the seeds and chop into 1cm dice.

Put the fish stock and white wine in a pan and cook until reduced, then whisk in the butter and add a squeeze of lemon juice. Set aside.

Heat a frying pan and pan-fry the seabass, skin-side down, until cooked.

Meanwhile, place the cockles and mussels into a hot pan, add the sauce and cook until they open. Discard any that do not open. Add the samphire and tomatoes.

Serve in a shallow bowl and top with the seabass.

Abel Heywood
EGGS ATLANTIC

After a night in the boutique hotel, this is one of the mouth-watering options that awaits on the breakfast menu. Serves 2.

Ingredients

6 eggs

A little butter

1 avocado

4 slices sourdough bread, toasted and buttered

180g smoked salmon

25g pea shoots

25g watercress

Method

Scramble the eggs slowly in a pan with a little butter. Halve, stone and peel the avocado, then slice it.

Serve the scrambled eggs on top of the sourdough toast with the smoked salmon and garnish with the sliced avocado, pea shoots and watercress.

Albert's STORY

Albert's Shed, Albert's Didsbury and Albert's Worsley comprise a unique family business that is based on delivering quality food to local customers.

The Albert's story began back in 2004, when Jim Ramsbottom opened his first restaurant in Castlefield with a simple aim that remains at the heart of the family business today: to serve quality food to local customers at a reasonable price in a sharp modern space with friendly, unpretentious service.

Jim's Uncle Albert, who led the conversion of Manchester food and drink institution Duke's 92 in the early 1990s, used to store his tools in the shed. When the ambitious plans were formed to transform the shed into a restaurant, Albert agreed to move his tools out on one condition… that the restaurant would retain the name of his beloved shed! Albert's Shed became established as one of Manchester's favourite dining destinations – a place where people receive a warm welcome, friendly service and consistently good-quality food and drink.

When two more restaurants followed within this family business, the Albert's name was so firmly associated with their core values that it was only natural to keep Uncle Albert in the name – so Albert's Restaurant and Bar opened in Didsbury in 2008, followed by Worsley in 2013.

What sets the Albert's name apart from other restaurants is the commitment to keeping those traditional family values at the heart of the business, which is consistently reflected in the ever-growing band of loyal regulars who choose to return to their local Albert's time after time.

Classic British food remains an integral part of each restaurant, but the menu is also peppered with inventive modern twists and a generous helping of flavourful Mediterranean dishes. Today the Italian classics, such as the antipasti sharing board and king prawn linguine is just as popular with the regulars as the much-loved Albert's fish and chips or the tender steaks, which are sourced from select Lancashire farms and dry-hung for a minimum of three weeks.

Of course Albert's is not just a restaurant – the bar is the ideal place to enjoy show-stopping cocktails or indulge in a glass (or bottle!) of Champagne. The atmosphere makes the perfect venue for private parties and events too.

By keeping the focus on quality local food and drink, warm service and a relaxed environment, this family-run success story looks set to continue retaining its devoted diners for many more years to come, as well as welcoming many new guests through its doors.

Albert's

Albert's
CHILLI PRAWN LINGUINI

A favourite Mediterranean seafood dish that will always impress guests.
Serves 2.

Ingredients

8-12 king prawns (140g)

1 tsp garlic, finely sliced

Add 40ml vegetable stock

2 small courgettes

1 sliced red pepper

8 cherry tomatoes, halved

Handful of flat Italian parsley, finely sliced

120g linguini, cooked

Handful of watercress

For the sauce:

20g butter

18g plain flour

A pinch of flaked chilli

40ml lemon juice

260ml vegetable stock

A pinch of white pepper

Method

As with all pasta, try and pick the best-quality fresh pasta and cook it in plenty of salted boiling water (1 dessert spoon of sea salt per 2 litres of water). If using dried pasta, use a good-quality durum wheat pasta and cook for 1 minute less than the suggested time on the packet. Drain thoroughly and immediately tip out on to a flat tray to cool, moving gently with a wooden spoon with a little extra virgin oil to stop it sticking. (Never cool it in water as this will wash away the carbohydrates from around the pasta, resulting in a loss of flavour.)

For the sauce, make a roux with the butter, flour and chilli and cook out to a blonde stage. A roux is a butter and flour base, cooked gently at the bottom of the pan and used to thicken sauces and add a rich background. Blonde stage is when the mixture turns a bright white colour and starts to produce a nutty aroma. This technique can be used in numerous sauces. Whisk in the lemon juice gradually and then the vegetable stock. Reduce to a simmer and cook out for 6-8 minutes until the sauce starts to thicken. Remove from heat, taste and adjust the seasoning.

Heat a frying pan with a little oil to just before it starts to smoke, add the prawns (use shell-on raw prawns to enhance the flavour) and colour on each side. Season and add the garlic, then immediately add the 40ml stock. Add 150ml of the sauce and the vegetables, then taste and adjust the seasoning. Add your fresh chopped herb at the last minute to retain the flavour. Add the cooked pasta to the sauce, toss and coat thoroughly with the sauce until piping hot. Serve immediately, topped with watercress.

Albert's
CHOO CHEE SEAFOOD CURRY

A taste of the exotic with monkfish, scallops, mussels and prawns in
a creamy curry sauce. Serves 2.

Ingredients

2 tbsp coconut cream

400ml tin of coconut milk

60ml veg stock

1 tsp palm sugar

4 2cm pieces of monkfish tail

4 cleaned scallops

8 cleaned mussels

4 large prawns peeled and cleaned,
tails still on

10g edamame beans

Handful of sugar snaps

3 spring onions,

1 pak choi, cut into quarters
lengthways

½ red pepper, sliced into strips

4 Thai basil leaves

Salt

Boiled jasmin rice or soft noodles
to serve

For the paste:

2 tsp cumin seeds

2 tsp coriander seeds

2 tsp lime leaves

3 tbsp galangal

2 tsp curry powder

2 tbsp tom yum paste

30g shallots

15g garlic

Method

Start by making the paste. Roughly chop all the paste ingredients and fry gently in a large saucepan with the spices. Once you can smell the aromatics start to release their flavour, add the coconut cream, coconut milk and most of the stock.

Simmer for 20 minutes then add the palm sugar and adjust the salt to taste. Blend until very smooth.

In a frying pan quickly colour the monkfish and the scallops and prawns, then set aside.

Add the mussels (beards removed, thoroughly cleaned and any open ones discarded) and a little of the stock, and bring to a brisk boil until all of the mussels are opened. Add the sauce and warm through. Once the sauce is hot, add the rest of the seafood. Be careful not to overcook the scallops and monkfish at this stage as they will become dry and chewy.

Just before you serve it, add the vegetables, which should be neatly cut, so they keep their structure and freshness – you don't want soggy vegetables!

Serve with boiled jasmine rice or soft noodles (we use a combination of different rice to add bite and flavour).

Note - when using dry spices, always check the date and make sure they have been kept in an air-tight container, as spices lose their aroma and flavour over time and this will affect the final result. This curry has quite a lot of texture even though it is blended, and this is exactly how it should be, as it adds to the body of the curry.

Albert's
CHOCOLATE VOLCANO

Here is a recipe for true chocoholics! Serves 4.

Ingredients

For the ganache:

55ml double cream

170g dark chocolate

60g butter, softened

30ml brandy

For the sponge:

315g chocolate

135g caster sugar

50g butter

4 large eggs

Seeds of 1 vanilla pod

50g plain flour

Method

Preheat the oven to 200°C.

For the ganache, place the chocolate in a stainless steel bowl and, in a separate pan, bring the cream gently to the boil. Pour the cream over the chocolate and stir until smooth and glossy. Finish with the softened butter and brandy, mixing thoroughly through the chocolate. Set aside.

For the sponge, melt the chocolate. Blend the sugar and butter together until pale and smooth. Beat the eggs together and mix into the creamed butter and sugar, along with the seeds from the vanilla pod. Gradually mix the chocolate into the egg and butter mixture, then fold in the flour, making sure it is completely incorporated.

Grease and lightly dust the moulds, then fill them one-third full with the sponge mixture. Add a large teaspoon of ganache, being careful to keep it away from the sides of the mould. Fill another third of the mould with sponge mixture (so it comes two-thirds up the pot in total). Bake in the oven for 10 minutes if the ganache is at room temperature or 9 minutes if the ganache is still slightly warm.

Dust the volcanoes with icing sugar, warm through the remaining ganache and pour some over to form a sauce. Garnish with sugared pecans and some honeycomb ice cream.

Spilling THE BEANS

Seasonal speciality coffee from around the world is being hand-roasted in the newly redeveloped area of Manchester – welcome to Ancoats Coffee Company.

Although he's always loved a good cup of coffee, it wasn't until he found himself working for a coffee company in Melbourne that Jamie Boland realised what an incredible variety there was to explore out there. He began working there simply to fund his travels, but soon he found himself captivated by the industry and he dedicated himself to learning about every aspect of the process from sourcing the best suppliers to the intricacies of roasting.

When Jamie arrived back in the UK, he set his sights on bringing the very finest coffee to the good caffeine-lovers of Manchester. He loved the gritty post-industrial charm of Ancoats. Once home to the first ever cotton mills, the cobbled streets ooze irresistible northern charm and the architectural heritage retains memories of Manchester's industrial past. Today, the sympathetic regeneration has seen this once important area thrive again, and it seemed the perfect area for Jamie to base his business.

Ancoats Coffee Company know everything there is to know about their beans. Ask Jamie about the country of origin, location, farm, altitude, coffee variety or processing methods and his knowledge is extensive. This is a man who not only

prides himself on the quality of his products, but is genuinely passionate about them too.

The beans are all hand-roasted in small batches and in complete view of the customer, actively engaging them in the roasting process from bean to cup. Roasting coffee is a science and, like any scientist, Jamie is continually experimenting with the process to improve his methods and learn new techniques. Coffee, like wine, is affected by a diverse range of factors such as terroir, microclimate, variety, altitude and processing method – with each country or region displaying distinct flavour characteristics. To maintain quality and consistency they 'cup' each roast, ensuring every batch meets the desired parameters or 'roast profile' for that coffee. Luckily, Ancoats Coffee Company has created a 'cupping chart' for each product to help give customers an idea of what flavour characteristics they can expect.

And this is all just the very beginning for this innovative local business. With Manchester waking up to the delights of speciality coffee roasted on their doorstep, they are going to be working hard to keep up with demand!

Ancoats Coffee Company
HOW TO USE AN AEROPRESS

This brewing method is very popular in speciality coffee circles. Loved by home-enthusiasts and professional baristas alike – it's an easy way to brew coffee, produces a lovely cup of coffee and is a great way to explore your curiosity further. There are a myriad of Aeropress recipes out there, which is testament to the versatility of the Aeropress itself. They are relatively inexpensive and easily found online or in your local speciality coffee shop. All the equipment required (except kettle, scales, grinder and cup) comes with the Aeropress.

Equipment

Aeropress filter papers (included)

Kettle (gooseneck if possible)

Digital weighing scales (essential)

Timer (essential)

Jug or wide-rimmed cup/mug (250ml+ in volume)

Thermometer (optional)

Coffee grinder (optional but highly recommended)

Method

I recommend using a speciality single origin such as Ancoats Coffee Co. Ethiopia Rocko Mountain Reserve Natural.

Use the brewing ratio: 18g coffee to 250g/ml water.

Fill the kettle and turn on. Whilst waiting for the kettle to boil, insert an aeropress filter paper into the filter cap holder and set aside for later.

Measure/weigh out your coffee beans and grind to medium-fine coarseness. Re-weigh the ground coffee to check there has been no 'loss'. If using pre-ground coffee, ensure this is of a medium-fine grind and weigh accordingly.

Insert the plunger into the bottom of the Aeropress (opposite end to the cap) and place it on a level surface, cap-side up. Add your ground coffee to the aeropress and shake gently to level out.

Once the kettle has boiled, allow to cool for a couple of minutes. (Coffee should ideally be brewed at around 85-90°C to help minimise any bitterness. If possible, use a thermometer to check the temperature.)

Place the Aeropress onto your digital scales and tare to zero. Take the filter cap holder and pour hot water over the filter paper to remove any paper taste. Gently pour enough hot water to cover the grounds and gently stir with the paddle, making sure all the grounds are wet. Wait 30 seconds to allow the coffee to 'bloom'.

Slowly add the rest of the water to the Aeropress so that the weighing scales show 250g (250ml). Stir gently. Wait 1 minute 30 seconds, then stir thoroughly.

Now attach the filter paper cap to the Aeropress, turn over and place on your serving vessel of choice (jug/cup/mug). Carefully press the plunger by placing your hand on top and applying force to get it moving. Aim to finish 'the press' in 20 seconds until you hear a 'hissing' sound. Serve and enjoy!

Pastries FROM PARIS

The art of French pastry is being preserved at Bisous Bisous, where a little taste of Paris is being welcomed by Didsbury locals.

When Alex Moreau and Kirsty McAlpine opened their little corner of Paris in Didsbury, they wanted to keep the traditional French values at its heart by providing authentic products prepared by hand using traditional methods. Entering the shop and casting your eye over the simply beautiful range of cakes, pastries and macarons on display and you can't fail to be astounded by what they achieve every day.

Bisous Bisous is more than a pâtisserie – it is a boulangerie, a Viennoiserie and a pâtisserie in one. Head Pastry Chef Olivier Stievenard is the man behind the stunning macarons and cakes. Beginning work at 2am every morning, alongside his team of dedicated and highly skilled chefs, he sets about creating the products through the early hours, so the aroma of freshly baked bread and croissants still warm from the oven are ready to greet the morning shoppers.

Delicious offerings such as éclairs, tartelettes, macarons, croissants, petit brioche and pain aux raisins are prepared alongside stunning gateaux and celebration cakes. Seasonality is embraced in the recipes, with soft summer fruits featuring over the summer and berries taking centre stage over the winter. During the Christmas period, the chefs enjoy creating heady festive flavours and using rich and indulgent ingredients like chocolate.

Kirsty enjoys catering for local residents and has been part of many a special occasion by developing dream cakes for parties, weddings and events. From a towering croquembouche to intricate wedding favours, she loves helping people incorporate a bit of French flair into their big day. One of their most popular requests is to create a cake table of various gateaux and tartes – although when the cakes are this beautiful, it almost seems a shame to cut into them!

Bisous Bisous
GATEAU OPERA

This is a classic layered French cake made with an almond sponge
cake known as joconde. Serves 6.

Ingredients

For the joconde sponge cake:

125g almond powder

125g icing sugar

35g plain flour

165g whole eggs

125g egg whites

25g caster sugar

30g butter, melted

For the coffee syrup:

100g caster sugar

100g water

80g coffee

For the coffee buttercream:

68g egg white

138g sugar

50g water

200g butter, softened

30g coffee extract

For the chocolate ganache:

132g cream

132g dark chocolate, 55%

35g butter

For the glaçage:

100g dark chocolate, 55%

40g butter

15g corn oil

Equipment:

60 x 40cm cake frame

18 x 3cm cake ring

Silpat mat or greaseproof paper

Method

Preheat the oven to 220°C.

For the joconde sponge, with a whisk beat together the almond powder, the icing sugar, the flour and the eggs. In another bowl beat the egg whites together with the caster sugar. In the first mixture gradually and delicately fold in the beaten egg whites and the butter that has been melted and is still warm. Line a sheet pan with greaseproof and place the cake frame on top. Pour in the mixture. Cook in the preheated oven for 8-10 minutes. Remove from the oven and let cool.

For the coffee syrup, boil the sugar and water until dissolved, then mix in the coffee until blended. Leave until the syrup is cool.

For the coffee buttercream, add the egg whites to your mixer and beat to soft peaks. Add the sugar and water to a saucepan and cook to 120°C. Add the melted sugar to the egg whites. Beat the mixture strongly on the 3rd setting, after 5 minutes add the softened butter and coffee extract.

For the chocolate ganache, heat the cream to near boiling, pour onto the chocolate and stir until it is a smooth texture. Incorporate the butter in small pieces.

For the glaçage, melt the chocolate and butter together, then gently incorporate the corn oil. Leave until tepid.

To build the cake, cut out three 18cm circles from the cooled joconde sponge. Place one layer of joconde sponge into the cake ring and soak with the coffee syrup. Add half of the coffee buttercream in a layer and another circle of joconde sponge on top. Soak this sponge layer with coffee syrup, pour ganache on top. Add the final layer of joconde sponge and soak with coffee syrup. Add the remainder of the coffee buttercream in a smooth layer, leave on side for 15 minutes before pouring on the glaçage. Place in the fridge for 1-2 hours to chill. Once set, remove from fridge. Using a knife heated in boiling water, slide the knife around the edge of the cake ring and slide the cake out.

Taking The
STARRING ROLE

The vibrant colours and extravagance of the Bollywood film industry makes this award-winning gem of a restaurant one of Manchester's most exciting places to enjoy modern Indian cooking, specialising in Halal food. A firm favourite with customers is the mouthwatering Samunder is a flavoursome medium spiced dish of king prawns, prawns and fish, cooked with garlic, ginger. and special Bollywood Masala spices then garnished with coriander.

Awarded Best Restaurant of the Year in the north-west by the Asian Curry Awards and the English Curry Awards in 2014, Bollywood Masala has been winning awards and local recognition for its outstanding curries.

A modern approach to Indian cooking is combined with using traditional ingredients and authentic spices, resulting in a contemporary menu with classic favourites and unique fusion dishes sitting side by side.

There is an intriguing array of mouthwatering dishes on the menu, which customers don't find at many traditional Indian restaurants.

The Bollywood Masala chefs are proud of their specialities which take in flavours from around the world and offer something that little bit different to the Manchester spice-lovers.

The specialities section of the menu is refreshingly long, so customers may find it difficult to choose between intriguing delights such as veeru, a Nepalese lamb curry which is heavy with a touch of cream and enjoyed in the bitter mountain winters of Nepal; muqaddar ka sikandar, a brunch-style dish of freshly prepared chicken, lamb, vegetables and daal served with rice and chapatti; and Katrina, a dish of shredded chicken marinated in yoghurt and red spices served in foil in a beautiful bird-shaped presentation.

Of course the classics are all cooked to perfection too, and if something is not on the menu the chefs will do their best to prepare something perfect to fit the bill. Nothing is too much trouble for the dedicated staff who go above and beyond to make every guest feel like a Bollywood celebrity.

Owner Gopal Tabak wants every customer to have an exhilarating experience when they dine at his restaurant, from the welcome and ambience to the food and service – and with awards under their belt and loyal customers returning time and time again, his success is speaking for itself.

Bollywood Masala

Understated EXCELLENCE

Simple, honest and seasonal fare cooked to the highest standards is the aim at Brassica Grill, which has quickly become not only one of Heaton Moor's hottest spots, but also one of Manchester's must-try dining destinations.

The light, modern interior of this popular restaurant offers a welcoming environment that instantly makes diners feel relaxed and reflects the classic simplicity of the food on the menu. The 45-seater restaurant in the heart of bustling Heaton Moor is owned by Paul Faulkner. Paul made his name in restaurants such as the Modern Restaurant at Urbis, Chester Grosvenor, where he trained for six years, L'Odeon, where his cooking style developed under the influence of Bruno Loubet, and the prestigious Harvey Nichols OXO Tower and Knightsbridge restaurants.

Not only have the reviews been fantastic, but this local gem has achieved a Michelin Bib Gourmand award for 2016 – an amazing accolade, which is the result of a huge amount of dedication to taking the best quality ingredients and simply cooking them well.

There is no fuss to the cooking at this award-winning restaurant. Instead, they have achieved recognition by taking the best ingredients and using classic cooking techniques and culinary flair to produce honest, high-quality fare. From potted smoked trout, ham hock terrine and piccalilli or Cornish fish soup to homity pie, ox cheek pudding or roast lemon sole, the kitchen at the Brassica Grill is celebrating British cooking at its best. As for its grills, for which it is famed (and named!), there is something for all appetites, from the 8oz fillet steak to the 12oz bacon chop, or why not go for the succulent 16oz T-bone steak.

Passionate about local and seasonal produce, Paul and fellow chef Matt O'Brien source all their ingredients from trusted suppliers, from whom they can be sure they're getting the best quality local meat, poultry, fish and vegetables. The seasons dictate the menu, which changes regularly depending on what is available, as well as to ensure that there is always something new on offer for the ever-growing band of loyal regulars.

Brassica Grill
ROAST RUMP OF HIGH PEAK LAMB

and Brassica broth.

We get the lamb for this dish from a small butchers in Glossop called Mettrick's, who I have used for all our lamb for quite a few years. All of Mettrick's lamb comes from the Peak District and he knows the farmers well. The lamb is bred on the hills in the Peak District, eating flowers, heather and the like, which gives it a really good flavour. Serves 4.

Ingredients

4 rumps of lamb

Olive oil, for cooking

A knob of butter, for cooking

For the broth:

4 Savoy cabbage leaves

200g carrots, peeled and cut into 1cm dice

200g turnip, peeled and cut into 1cm dice

200g swede, peeled and cut into 1cm dice

200g parsnips, peeled and cut into 1cm dice

100g onion, peeled and cut into 1cm dice

100g celery, peeled and cut into 1cm dice

100ml white wine

200g potato, peeled and cut into 1cm dice

1 litre chicken or lamb stock

Salt and ground black pepper

1 bay leaf

Olive oil, for cooking

Method

In a large heavy-based pan, sweat off the cabbage leaves in olive oil. Add the diced carrots, turnip, swede, parsnips, onion and celery and season well. Cover and cook until the vegetables begin to soften.

Turn up the heat, and add white wine and reduce. Add the stock to cover and cook until the vegetables are almost cooked, then add the potato and simmer until cooked. This can be made in advance – it will improve when left to go cold and reheated.

Preheat the oven to 180°C.

Season the lamb rumps with salt and pepper. Put a splash of olive oil in a hot ovenproof frying pan, add the lamb and colour the lamb all over. Add a knob of butter and cook in the preheated oven for around 10-12 minutes, depending on size, until cooked to your liking.

Allow to rest for 10 minutes, then carve each into three even pieces. Put any roasting juices into the broth.

Reheat the broth, if necessary. Put a large ladle of the broth into each bowl and serve the lamb on top.

The Only Bury Black Pudding
ON THE BLOCK

The only Bury black puddings to be made in Bury today, The Bury Black Pudding Company proves that the north West is still making some of the finest black puddings in the UK.

Debbie Pierce began her black pudding story at the age of 12, working as a Saturday girl on Bury Market for James Wallace, a farmer who was one of the longest standing traders on the market. When James retired, Debbie took over the stall, which was supplied with black puddings by Jack and Richard Morris. Jack retired around the same time and his son Richard took over the black pudding production, setting in motion a journey that would see the dedicated pair taking this great northern delicacy from its market stall beginnings to a nationwide operation.

It was Debbie's shrewd business mind that saw the opportunity to expand the flourishing business from its popular market stall. As soon as she saw the emergence of online food websites, she made sure that The Bury Black Pudding Company would be part of this new trend. As a result, she not only increased sales but built awareness of the brand incredibly quickly, getting their products into national supermarkets like Asda, Tesco, Sainsbury's, Morrisons, Waitrose and the Co-op.

Although the highly successful product is now sold through all the big high street supermarkets, the market stall at Bury market is still at the heart and soul of the company. Many long-standing staff have remained employed at the family-run business for years, and the company now employs about 70 people in the Bury area. On the factory floor, the traditional recipe and production methods remain very much the same, providing the hand-finished quality product that the customers know and love.

What is inside these black puddings that has kept them a cut above the competition? As they specialise in making black puddings, you can be assured that only the very best quality ingredients are sourced and their individual selection of herbs & spices used in the recipe creates their own unique flavour. With no artificial ingredients or preservatives, along with being low in fat and high in iron, all this makes it a very healthy product too.

Although the traditional black and white puddings remain extremely popular, Debbie and Richard are always keen to explore new products and opportunities for expansion. With exciting new products such as chilli black pudding and the fantastic gluten-free black pudding joining the classic recipes, this forward-thinking company is embracing the future while keeping the heritage of Bury's favourite product at its heart.

Now supplying over 12 countries around the world, The Bury Black Pudding Company are bringing this northern delicacy to the masses, whilst still maintaining all of its traditional values.

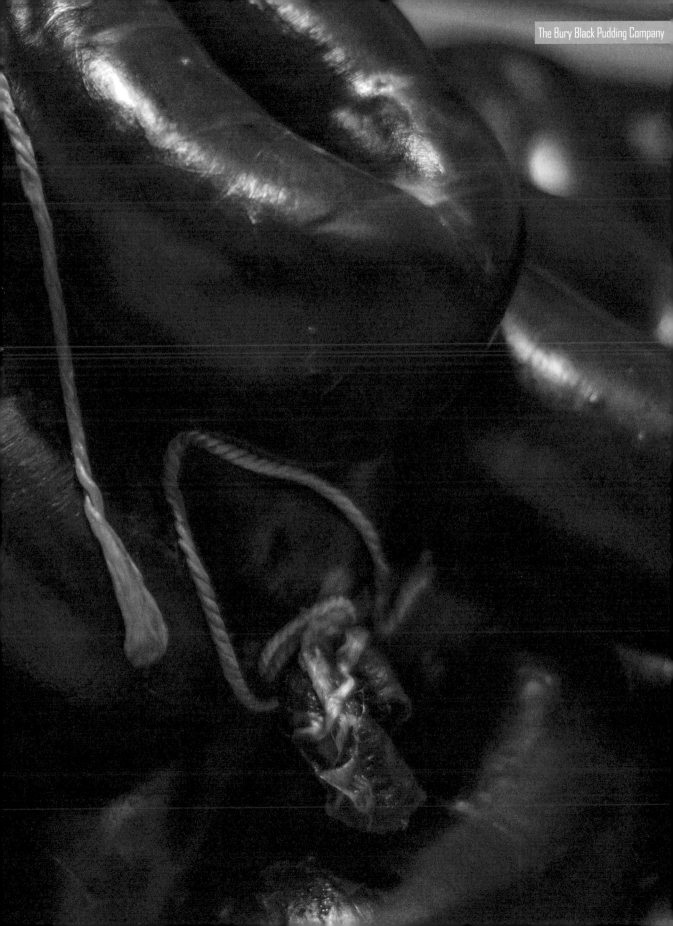

The Bury Black Pudding Company
LAMB HOT POT WITH BLACK PUDDING

A Lancashire classic with the delicious addition of Bury Black Pudding.
Serves 4.

Ingredients

2 tbsp olive oil

1kg lamb neck, chopped

2 onions, sliced

½ tsp salt

1 tbsp plain flour

200ml lamb stock

1 sprig of fresh thyme

2 bay leaves

1 tbsp Worcestershire sauce

50g butter, cubed

2 x 200g Bury Black Pudding Rings, sliced and skin removed

1kg potatoes, peeled and sliced

Salt and pepper

Method

Preheat the oven to 180°C.

Heat the oil in a pan and fry the lamb for a few minutes to brown. Remove from the pan and set aside. In the same pan, cook the onions for 2-3 minutes, then season with the salt. Stir in the flour. Add the stock a little at a time, then add the thyme, bay leaves and Worcestershire sauce. Stir and simmer for 8-10 minutes.

Grease a lidded casserole dish and place a layer of potatoes over the bottom of the dish. Season well. Spoon in half the browned lamb, then arrange half the black pudding slices on top. Pour over half the onion and stock liquid. Repeat the layering process until you have used up all the ingredients, making sure you finish with a top layer of potatoes.

Dot the top layer of potatoes with the butter, then cover with a lid and cook in the preheated oven for 20 minutes.

Remove the lid and cook for a further 20 minutes uncovered. Serve with your favourite vegetables.

From the Farm
TO THE CITY

A shining example of how to bring fresh products from the local countryside into the heart of a city, The Butcher's Quarter in Manchester has brought the oink, moo, cluck and baa to the Northern Quarter.

Housed in an old butcher's shop, Manchester's new inner-city butcher is bridging the gap between the old and the new – the original butcher's plaque on the wall being one of the only giveaways to its historic past, while the modern interior oozes contemporary Northern Quarter charm.

Owner Steve Pilkington spent two years researching the best local produce before opening the shop, and his commitment to sourcing local meat is evident through his whole range. The beef is from the Peak District, the chicken is from Highbury, the lamb is from Helmshore and the pork is from Rossendale – all free-range and reared within 20 miles of the Northern Quarter.

The friendly service and welcoming environment go hand in hand with this ethos – not only will the knowledgeable staff be able to tell you exactly where the meat is from, they are also happy to offer advice on cuts and cooking techniques.

Today's busy lifestyles often require something quick and easy to cook, but the team at The Butcher's Quarter have made sure none of us have to rely on poor-quality ready meals for a quick fix, as they offer a mouth-watering selection of ready-to-cook meats that are marinated and full of flavour. You can also pick up a 'breakfast pack' for your fry-up – the perfect portion of sausages, bacon and eggs ready to pop into the pan.

Charcuterie and cheeses can be bought here too – the cheeses have been selected from specialist supplier J. J. Sandham in Lancashire, who use milk from local farms and know everything there is to know about all things dairy.

So, you've picked up your breakfast bacon, your Sunday roasting joint, your midweek meat and some delicious hams and cheeses… now to finish off your shopping with a bottle of carefully selected wine from some of the finest producers.

The Butcher's Quarter is about much more than meat. It's about bringing the best locally sourced food together in one place. The team have done all the research for you – all you have to do is pop in, say hello and choose from the incredible food and drink on offer.

Butcher's Quarter
VENISON STEAK

with beetroot, black pudding and a juniper sauce
Looking for something special for the weekend? Can we suggest... Serves 4.

Ingredients

4 venison steaks, approximately 175g each

Olive oil

4 slices of black pudding, approximately 1 cm thick

20g butter

Salt and black pepper

For the juniper sauce:

Some venison bones

35g butter

1 tbsp olive oil

½ carrot, chopped

½ small onion, chopped

½ celery stick, chopped

100ml red wine

1 tbsp redcurrant jelly

250 ml veal jus (made from boiling bones and vegetables for 4 hours before straining and then reducing to about one-quarter)

1 tbsp crusted juniper berries

1 bouquet garni

A few cubes of butter, to glaze

To serve:

Beetroot, boiled and grated

Potato galette (potato spaghetti, fried and browned)

Method

Season the venison and coat in olive oil, then leave to marinate for an hour. Whilst this is marinating, make the sauce.

Brown the venison bones in the butter and the oil in a large pan. Add the carrot, onion and celery and cook until browned, then pour in the wine and add the redcurrant jelly. Cook until reduced to a syrup. Combine with the veal jus, juniper berries and bouquet garni, and simmer until the sauce thickens. Strain and season to taste.

Sear the marinated venison on both sides in olive oil in a hot pan before putting it in the oven for 4 minutes. It should be springy but not soft. Let it rest for 5 minutes, covered in foil.

Whilst the venison is resting, fry both sides of the black pudding in the butter.

Ensure the beetroot, potato and sauce are re-heated to serving temperature. Add small cubes of butter to the sauce to glaze. Slice the venison and place on top of the black pudding, serve with the beetroot and potato galette on the side. Drizzle with the sauce.

A Pizza the
ACTION

Having celebrated the fifteenth anniversary of its first restaurant in November 2015, the pioneering independent Manchester restaurant group Croma remains one of Manchester's brightest businesses.

Croma symbolises, for many, what Manchester independent eateries are all about. When the first restaurant opened its doors in 2000 on Clarence Street in Manchester city centre, few could have anticipated the successes that would be in store for this gourmet pizzeria.

As restaurants in Chorlton, Prestwich and Didsbury followed, Croma has maintained the originality that set it apart from the competition at the turn of the century. The stylish designs of each restaurant are all thanks to the legendary 93-year-old Italian designer Enzo Apicella. The original designer in the 1960s for the first Pizza Express venues, Enzo continues to set each restaurant apart with individual designs.

Three years running (2011, 2012 and 2013) Croma was voted most family-friendly restaurant at the Manchester Food & Drink Awards. It appears in the Trip Advisor Excellence 'Hall of Fame' with consistently good reviews for 5 years running. Most recently it has been selected by The Sunday Times in The UK Dining Out Guide as one of the top 10 best value restaurants in the north-west.

What makes the dining experience so special? The beautiful setting and dedicated service are certainly excellent, but the commitment to quality, locally sourced ingredients and innovative menus continue to keep Croma at the top of the Manchester food and drink scene. Whether you opt for an Italian classic pizza such as the marinara or the fiorentina or try one from the gourmet selection such as the tandoori chicken or garstang blue, you can always rely on fine pizzas baked in specially imported ovens.

And with a lunch menu, an early bird menu and a children's menu on offer, there are plenty of opportunities to take advantage of all that lovely deliciousness at exceptionally good value. Watch out for their exciting new venture in partnership with Odeon cinemas, when the innovative "pizza-at-the-movies" offer opens at the Trafford Centre in December – it seems there is no stopping these dedicated Manchester pizza-lovers.

Croma
AGLEFINO PIZZA

One of Croma's most popular pizza combinations – free-range egg and natural smoked haddock. This is perfect for brunch or any time of day. Serves 1.

Ingredients

170g dough

56g crème fraiche (1½ dessert spoons)

14g leeks, chopped

86g smoked haddock, broken into chunks

42g Emmental

A dash of lemon juice

Oregano

5ml olive oil

1 egg

3g chopped parsley

Lemon wedge

Salt and black pepper

For the dough:

500g '00' Flour

7g fast-acting yeast

325ml warm water

1 tbsp caster sugar

1.5 tbsp olive oil

Method

For the dough, sieve the flour into a mixing bowl and add the salt. Make a well for the liquids. Mix the yeast with the warm water, sugar and oil. Leave for 1-2 minutes. Stir the yeast liquid into the flour using a fork until it becomes easier to mix by hand and more dough-like. Empty the dough onto a floured surface and knead for 3-4 minutes. Put into a clean, lightly oiled mixing bowl and cover with cling flim. Leave in a warm place for 1 hour or until it has risen to double its size.

Place back onto a floured surface and knead for another minute to knock the air out. You will have enough for two large pizzas or four smaller ones. (Any excess can be stored in the refrigerator for up to 2 days. Allow to stand for 2 hours at room temperature before making pizzas.)

Preheat the oven to 190°C.

Roll out the dough to the required size and place on a large baking tray. Spread the crème fraîche over the pizza with the back of a spoon.

Add the leeks to the base, followed by the pieces of haddock, leaving a space in the centre (10cm) for the egg.

Distribute the Emmental evenly over the pizza (not in the centre). Add the lemon juice. Season with black pepper and oregano, and drizzle with olive oil.

Cook in the hot oven for about 7 minutes and remove. Crack the egg into the centre of the pizza and return to the oven until the pizza is golden brown or the egg is cooked to your liking. Garnish with chopped parsley and a lemon wedge.

Croma
FUNGHI DI BOSCO PIZZA

A beautiful and rich-tasting twist on the classic mushroom pizza. Serves 1.

Ingredients

170g dough

70g tomato sauce/passata

21g field mushrooms, sliced

21g Paris brown mushrooms, sliced

57g mozzarella, cubed

21g oyster mushrooms, torn

Oregano

3ml garlic oil

Fresh rosemary sprig

2ml truffle oil 2ml (if concentrate, dilute with five parts extra virgin olive oil)

Salt and pepper

For the dough:

500g '00' Flour

1 tsp fine salt

7g fast-acting yeast

325ml warm water

1 tbsp caster sugar

1.5 tbsp olive oil

Method

For the dough, sieve the flour into a mixing bowl and add the salt. Make a well for the liquids. Mix the yeast with the warm water, sugar and oil. Leave for 1-2 minutes. Stir the yeast liquid into the flour using a fork until it becomes easier to mix by hand and more dough-like. Empty the dough onto a floured surface and knead for 3-4 minutes. Put into a clean, lightly oiled mixing bowl and cover with cling flim. Leave in a warm place for 1 hour or until it has risen to double its size.

Place back onto a floured surface and knead for another minute to knock the air out. You will have enough for two large pizzas or four smaller ones. (Any excess can be stored in the refrigerator for up to 2 days. Allow to stand for 2 hours at room temperature before making pizzas.)

Preheat the oven to 190°C.

Roll out the dough to the required size and place on a large baking tray. Spread the tomato sauce over the pizza base with a ladle.

Arrange the mushrooms over the sauce without overlapping. Distribute the mozzarella cubes evenly over the pizza. Season with salt, black pepper and oregano.

Drizzle with garlic oil and sprinkle with fresh rosemary. Cook in the hot oven until golden brown. Finish with a dash of truffle oil before serving.

Croma
CROMA MARTINI

Made with Chambord, a French liquor. This martini is a sweet infusion of black and red raspberries, Madagascar vanilla and XO cognac and has proved a popular choice for the cocktail connoisseur. Serves 1.

Ingredients

1 shot (25ml) vodka

1 shot (25ml) Chambord

A dash of sweet martini

A slug of strawberry juice

A squeeze of fresh lime juice

Ice

Method

Mix the vodka, martini dash, Chambord and strawberry juice with ice in a cocktail shaker. Squeeze in the juice of half a fresh lime. Shake well and strain into a chilled martini glass. Garnish with lime slice.

Tea Time TREATS

Cupcakes, layer cakes, brownies, traybakes, slices, scones, desserts and puddings... life is sweet in West Didsbury when you visit And the Dish Ran Away with the Spoon.

Dutch-born Annemiek grew up surrounded by a love of sweet things. A wooden spoon in her hand from an early age, she spent her childhood helping her mother make (and eat!) delicious desserts. As an adult, she began to work in a bakery in Amsterdam, where she was trained by American baker 'Dan the Cookie Man', who soon helped her transform her natural flair for baking into a lifelong passion.

When Annemiek moved to the UK, she took on the role as manager at And the Dish Ran Away with the Spoon and immediately fell in love with its unique charm, incredible cakes and its dedication to making tea time something extra special. After 3 years, when the opportunity arose to purchase the thriving little café, Annemiek was delighted.

Since she has owned And the Dish Ran Away with the Spoon, Annemiek has kept the quality of ingredients at the core of the business – the finest teas and coffees, and the very best home-made cakes. It's no surprise this West Didsbury favourite featured in The Independent's top 50 tea rooms in the UK.

With high chairs, baby-changing facilities and toys for the little ones, the warm and welcoming environment is perfect for busy mums or an after-school treat during the week, and it's ideal for a catch up with friends at the weekend over a lazy afternoon tea. The team also caters for weddings and parties, and they can create show-stopping cake and dessert tables for any occasion.

Although you'll find the British classics on the cake stands, Annemiek likes to try new things on the menu each week. An avid follower of blogs and new trends, you can be sure that she is always testing new recipes and experimenting with flavours from around the world. Her American-style brownies are one of the most popular treats with her regulars. In fact, so popular that she developed a sister company The Brownie Post (www.thebrowniepost.co.uk) to deliver her gooey goodies to people around the UK – excellent news for those who live too far away from Didsbury to get their brownie fix!

Dish and Spoon
STRAWBERRY ETON MESS CAKE

This recipe makes 12 big wedges. You could cut it into smaller portions, if you like, but that's the way we like to serve it in the café! Serves 12.

Ingredients

For the cake:

375g plain flour

1 tsp salt

1 tbsp baking powder

125ml sour cream

125ml buttermilk

2 tsp vanilla extract

225g unsalted butter, at room temperature

450g caster sugar

4 medium eggs

For the icing:

250g mascarpone cheese

60g icing sugar

250ml double cream

1½ tsp vanilla extract

For the meringue and decoration:

2 medium egg whites

110g white caster sugar

A handful of strawberries

Good-quality strawberry jam or conserve (we love Wild and Fruitful, Cumbria)

Fresh mint leaves

Method

Preheat the oven to 180°C.

Grease and line the bases and sides of two deep, round, 20cm loose-bottomed cake tins with baking parchment.

In a small bowl, mix the flour, salt and baking powder together with a whisk. Mix together the sour cream, buttermilk and vanilla in a small jug. Beat the butter and sugar together with an electric hand whisk for a few minutes until light and fluffy. Add the eggs one at a time and beat until fully incorporated.

Using an electric mixer on a low speed, mix together the dry ingredients and buttermilk mixture in small amounts, alternating between the two. Use a spatula to scrape the mixture from the sides of the bowl and continue to mix until no more flour is visible.

Divide the mixture between the two cake tins. Smooth and flatten the mixture without pushing it right to the edges of the tins.

Bake in the preheated oven for 30-40 minutes, checking after 20 minutes in case it needs a foil hat to stop it from browning too much. You will know when the cakes are done when a cocktail stick inserted into the middle comes out clean.

Reduce the oven to 100°C.

Let the cakes cool a little in the tins before taking them out and putting them onto a wire rack to cool completely.

For the icing, whisk the mascarpone and icing sugar together until smooth. Then add the double cream and continue to whisk until stiff peaks form. It should be thick, but smooth and glossy. Add the vanilla and fold it in gently.

For the meringue, beat the egg whites until they are stiff, on a low speed at first and then on high. Once they form stiff peaks you can slowly start adding the sugar, one spoonful at a time. Once all the sugar has been incorporated, continue to mix for a further few minutes until glossy and stiff.

Spoon the meringue mixture into a piping bag and squeeze little dollops onto a baking tray lined with parchment paper. This recipe will make more than you need for the cake, but you can snack on the rest (baker's perks!). Bake at 100°C for 45 minutes. If they are still soft, leave them in and keep checking them at 10 minute intervals. They are ready when they lift off the parchment easily. Remove and let cool on the baking tray.

To assemble the cake, spread half the icing onto one of the cakes. Drizzle a few spoonfuls of jam onto the icing, then place the other cake layer on top. Spread the other half of the icing onto the top of the cake and again, drizzle some jam over it. Top the cake with some halved strawberries, mint leaves and the meringues, some broken and some kept whole. Serve in big wedges and enjoy!

Bean to bar
CHOCOLATE

Dormouse Chocolates is creating hand-made chocolate bars, truffles and other confections that are being snapped up by the city's chocoholics.

From a Christmas temp in a luxury chocolate shop to Manchester's first bean-to-bar chocolatier, it's been quite a journey for Isobel Carse. Drawn into the indulgent world of chocolate-making, Isobel trained to become a professional chocolatier, learning not only the practical skills but also studying the fascinating history of cocoa and chocolate.

Not one to shy away from a challenge (Isobel had made her own wedding cake!), she took the plunge to open Dormouse Chocolates, and her products were embraced by the sweet-toothed Manchester locals at once.

The irresistible aroma sees queues of customers lining up for her hand-crafted products at the Makers Markets in Cheadle, Spinningfields, The Northern Quarter and Knutsford, as well as popular Chorlton Green Market. Collaborating with other traders, Isobel's range includes plenty of local ingredients that reflect Manchester's incredible food scene. She creates custom orders for bespoke products, too – simply choose a flavour and Dormouse Chocolates will create something special just for you.

Dormouse Chocolates
SIMPLE CHOCOLATE TRUFFLES

Makes 35-40.

Ingredients

225g dark chocolate (we love using Ecuadorian 70%)

250ml whipping cream

55g unsalted butter, chopped into small pieces

Cocoa powder or tempered chocolate, to finish

Method

Melt the chocolate gently in a bain-marie or heatproof bowl, set over a pan of gently simmering water until completely liquid.

While the chocolate is melting, heat the cream in a pan until it boils, then allow to cool slightly. Remove the chocolate from the heat and add the cream. Whisk together gently and add the butter until everything is combined into a smooth, shiny mixture.

Cover with cling film and place in the fridge to cool, until the mixture reaches the consistency of butter icing. As soon as it reaches this consistency, pipe or spoon the mixture into cherry-sized balls.

Cool for at least 2 hours then either roll in cocoa powder or dip in tempered chocolate.

Bienvenue à CHORLTON

In the heart of Chorlton, the independent deli, wine merchant and grocer Epicerie Ludo is the essential place to grab the finest local food and drinks, as well as some continental luxuries.

Four years since opening its doors on Beech Road, this popular little fine food store has been increasing its range of local products and top-quality imports to keep up with the demands of its loyal band of regular customers. Owner Ludovic, whose charming accent immediately gives away his French birthplace, is as passionate about his south Manchester home as he is about his French heritage. And this winning combination is what has made Epicerie Ludo such a success with the discerning shoppers of Chorlton.

In France, an epicerie is a grocery store, usually a small local shop which serves the community. As soon as you enter Epicerie Ludo it is clear that he has taken the French ideal of fine produce but given it a distinctly local feel. Everywhere you look you can see top-quality goodies from Manchester-based suppliers, hand-picked for their quality.

Ludovic is touched by the incredible support he has received from the community in this vibrant south Manchester suburb. He knows most of his customers by name and he finds lots of them pop in for a chat while they are picking up a bottle of wine or an essential ingredient for supper. Being open until 10pm enables people to visit after a long day at work, providing the convenience that is usually reserved for larger supermarkets.

People often ask Ludovic to source ingredients from around Europe, and he will always try to find those special luxuries from France, Spain, Italy or beyond. The wines have been carefully selected from around the world and there is a fine array of quality continental delicacies from across Europe that sit alongside the very best of British produce.

From freshly baked baguettes to traditional British cheeses, and from classic Italian Chianti to English sparkling wine, the one thing that unites this treasure trove of goodies is that you can rely on them all to be truly and utterly delicious.

Epicerie Ludo

Epicerie Ludo
TARTE FLAMBEE

A traditional recipe from the Alsace, this is the ideal dish to put together using the finest quality ingredients from Epicerie Ludo. Treat yourself to a bottle of fine wine to accompany it too. Why not try a lightly chilled bottle from the Alsace, a Pinot Blanc or a Pinot Gris for instance? Serves 2-4.

Ingredients

1 medium-sized thin pizza base (we use a Don Marco Pizza Base, which is sold in the shop)

80ml (2 large heaped tbsp) crème fraiche or sour cream

60g Emmental or Munster cheese

½ small brown onion (approx. 40g), finely chopped

65g smoked or unsmoked pancetta or bacon lardons

Ground black pepper, to season

Method

Pre-heat oven to 200°C (180°C fan).

Place the pizza base on a baking tray and cover evenly with the crème fraiche or sour cream. Grate the Emmental or crumble the Munster and sprinkle evenly over the crème fraiche or sour cream.

Sprinkle the finely chopped onion on top, and then sprinkle the pancetta or lardons liberally over the tarte. Finally season with a little black pepper.

Place the tarte in the pre-heated oven and bake for approximately 10 minutes, ensuring the cheese has started to bubble and the tarte has turned a light golden brown.

Epicerie Ludo
BAIE CHOCOLAT PASSION

This cocktail is fruity, warming and chocolatey, and it simply needs to be stirred together over ice. Serves 1.

Ingredients

25ml Mondino

25ml Sipsmith Sloe Gin

25ml Belsazar Red Vermouth

3 dashes of Chocolate Monin Bitters

Method

Fill a clean Boston glass to the top with nice, square, thick ice cubes. Measure and pour all the ingredients into the glass, except for the chocolate bitters.

Stir down for 10 seconds then add the chocolate bitters and stir for another 10 seconds.

Pour into a thin brandy glass, filled with ice cubes. Garnish with apple to bring out the fruits and spices of all ingredients. Bon Appétit!

By GEORGE!

A welcome new addition to the West Didsbury pub scene, the George Charles
has won over the locals through its simple focus on top-quality drinks and
home-cooked food.

There is no escaping the history of this characterful Victorian pub, which has established itself quickly and firmly in the hearts of the West Didsbury residents since it opened in September 2015. After doing a little research into the background of the building, its new owners, Mike Johnson and David Vanderhook named it The George Charles after an Armenian man who, after marrying an English girl, opened an exotic fruit shop in the premises in the 1890s.

The history hasn't just been preserved in the name; the Victorian heritage has been celebrated throughout and incorporated into modern designs, such as the unique feature wall which contains ten different styles of Victorian cornicing. It's this attention to detail and carefully considered balance between preserving the old and embracing the new which has created such a charming environment.

Lots of attention has been given to the drink selection, with a superb range of craft beers as well as fine wines and creative cocktails. The small kitchen is dedicated to creating top-quality food, from brunch through to evening meals. Head chef Andy McGann moved from the Manchester favourite Lime Bar in Salford Quays to head up the kitchen, and with many years of experience in London and Manchester under his belt, he is bringing high standards of cooking and creativity to the table.

Everything is cooked from scratch here and the menu changes regularly depending on what the seasons and local suppliers have to offer. With a firm focus on keeping the regulars at the heart of the business, the team are making sure that there is always something fresh and exciting on try. A plethora of inventive vegetarian options are a world away from the usual tried-and-tested offerings, and the freshly made Sunday roasts are proving to be a real hit with the locals. By putting good food at the heart of the community pub, the George Charles is fast becoming a cherished jewel in West Didsbury's gleaming crown.

The George
CHOCOLATE ORANGE FONDANT

A scoop of salted caramel ice cream goes very well with these fondants, along with a few strawberries to garnish. Serves 4.

Ingredients

5 eggs

5 egg yolks

175g sugar

500g chocolate, 70%

175g plain flour, sifted

25g cocoa, sifted

Zest of 1 orange

Seeds of 1 vanilla pod

25g melted butter

For coating the cups:

50g melted butter

Cocoa

Method

Chill 4 large cappuccino cups, brush with melted butter and chill again. After 15 minutes re-butter the cups and then coat with cocoa. Tap out the excess.

Preheat the oven to 180°C.

Mix the eggs and egg yolk together in mixer with a whisk.

Put the sugar in a pan and add 50ml water. Bring to the boil and simmer for 5 minutes to dissolve the sugar.

Slowly pour the melted sugar into the whisked eggs. Keep whisking until light and fluffy.

Melt the chocolate over a hot water bath.

Pour the melted chocolate into the egg mixture, then slowly add the sifted flour and cocoa, the vanilla seeds, orange zest and melted butter.

Fully combine all the ingredients, divide into the prepared cups and place on a tray in the preheated oven. Cook for exactly 12 minutes. Turn the fondants onto a plate to serve.

Bold As BRASS

Put down those shopping bags, take a seat and be dazzled by the food, drinks and service at Harvey Nichols Manchester Second Floor Bar and Brasserie.

Tucked away on the Second Floor, the chic dining space within the famous Harvey Nichols Manchester has long been a place for foodies in the know to savour a bite to eat or a refreshing cocktail during a day of hitting Manchester's impressive array of shops. A world away from the hustle and bustle outside, the ambience that greets you is serene, stylish and relaxing.

From being shown to your table to paying the bill, the members of staff are smart and attentive and strive for friendly and efficient service. Whether it's a glass of wine and a few sharing plates or a leisurely lunch over the whole afternoon, each diner is made to feel at ease.

The seasonally changing menu celebrates unusual flavours from around the world. For those who can't decide what mood their taste buds are in, you can select a varied mix of small plates – think Beef fillet carpaccio (served with brioche croutons, pickles and cep mustard), West Coast oysters (with Tabasco and lemon) or Hoi sin duck buns (with pickled cucumber and chilli).

Steaks are cooked to perfection on the Josper, an enclosed barbeque that retains irresistible flavours and aromas along with all the natural meat juices, which makes sure that the 28-day aged beef from John Holcroft's Farm in Cheshire is served at its absolute best. Alongside seasonal main courses, the Harvey Nichols classics remain ever-popular, too, with the Fish and chips, Burger and Niçoise salad remaining firmly with the favourites section. The effortlessly elegant desserts range from classic Tiramisu or Carrot cake to creative combinations such as Dandelion and burdock cake or Rice pudding dim sum.

One thing is for certain, no visit to the Second Floor Bar and Brasserie would be complete without indulging in one of their famous cocktails from the award-winning Bar – try the herbal flavours of Garden of Eden or the Mediterranean-inspired La Famiglia. Of course, you may just want to sit and watch the world go by with a glass of Champagne, spend a lazy day over Afternoon Tea or stay late in the evening sampling the various spirits from around the world. Whatever your mood, Harvey Nichols Manchester is the place to relax and indulge.

Second Floor Brasserie
TANDOORI MONKFISH

with aloo gobi and sticky mango rice.
A favourite dish on the menu, the warming spices complement
the sweet and sticky rice. Serves 4.

Ingredients

For the aloo gobi:

150g salt

1 cauliflower head, cut into small florets

15 whole cashews, pre-soaked in hot water for 20 minutes

1 tbsp butter

1 tbsp vegetable oil

10g cinnamon

1 bay leaf

3 green cardamom pods

3 cloves

500g diced onion

20g root ginger, peeled and diced

20g garlic, peeled and diced

500g tomatoes, chopped

10g chilli powder (Kashmiri if possible)

20g coriander powder

20g turmeric

250g Maris Piper potatoes, diced

20g garam masala

½ tsp crushed kasuri methi

Salt and pepper

For the sticky mango rice:

250g pilaf rice

30g mango chutney

For the tandoori monkfish:

140-160g monkfish tail per person (all skin, bone and sinew removed)

Tandoori powder

A pinch of Maldon salt

30ml vegetable oil

To serve:

Greek yoghurt

Micro coriander

Method

For the aloo gobi, add 500ml water to a small pan, add the salt and bring to the boil. Prepare the cauliflower into small florets and soak in the salty water for 20 minutes. Blend the soaked cashews to a smooth paste. Heat the butter and vegetable oil in a pan and add the cinnamon, bay leaf, green cardamom pods and cloves. Pan-fry the spice mix until it becomes aromatic, add the chopped onions to the pan and sauté until brown. Add the ginger and garlic, and cook until the aromas evaporate. Next add the finely chopped tomatoes and continue to cook for a further 5-7 minutes on a medium heat. Add the cashew paste, chilli powder, coriander and turmeric, turning the heat down to simmer for 8 minutes. Add the gobi (cauliflower,) aloo (potatoes) and 500ml water, season to taste. Cook for 40 minutes on a low heat with a lid on until the mixture turns creamy. Add the garam masala and methi leaves to finish.

For the sticky mango rice, wash the rice in cold water until the water runs clear. Place the rice in a saucepan with double the amount of water and bring to the boil. Turn the heat all the way down, covering the pan tightly with a lid. Cook on the lowest heat for 10 minutes without uncovering the pan. Once the rice is cooked, mix with the mango chutney and season to taste.

For the monkfish tandoori, preheat the oven for 200°C (fan 180°C). Roll the monkfish tail in tandoori powder and a pinch of salt until completely coated, adding a light glazing of vegetable oil. Leave to marinate for a minimum of 2 hours in the fridge. Add the remaining oil to an oven-proof pan and pan-fry the coated monkfish on a medium heat for 4-6 minutes until lightly brown, constantly turning the fish. Place the pan into the preheated oven for approximately 6-8 minutes. The monkfish texture should be firm but not hard. Slice the monkfish tail whilst hot.

Place a spoonful of Greek yoghurt onto the side of each plate. Pull the edge of the spoon through the yoghurt creating a smear on the plate. Take two spoons of the same size and take a scoop of the sticky mango rice. Pass the mixture between the spoons, turning and smoothing each side until a quenelle is formed. Place the quenelle of rice onto each plate. Repeat this four times leaving a gap between each quenelle. Add a spoonful of aloo gobi between each quenelle and gently position the tandoori monkfish tail on top. Finish each portion with a handful of micro-coriander to taste.

Second Floor Brasserie
ASSIETTE OF HONEY

The Manchester Bee is symbolised in this stunning dessert. To make this recipe at home, you'll need parchment paper, a piping bag, moulds for the mousse, a deep-fryer, a sugar thermometer and an ice cream machine. Serves 5.

Ingredients

For the honeycomb:
325g caster sugar
50g runny honey
125g glucose
60g water
15g bicarbonate of soda

For honeycomb mousse:
300g whipping cream
5 egg yolks
60g caster sugar
6g or 1 leaf gelatine, soaked in water
200g honeycomb
25g runny honey

For the chocolate soil:
95g butter
30g cocoa powder
95g plain flour
115g caster sugar
1g salt

For the loukoumades:
250g plain flour
1 tsp salt
12g fresh yeast
1 tbsp runny clear honey
250g warm water
Vegetable oil, for frying
Ground cinnamon

For the loukoumades sauce:
100g runny clear honey
1 tbsp soft light brown sugar
Juice and zest of ½ lemon
20g butter
1 tbsp water

For the pistachio paste:
100g caster sugar
100g water
250g shelled pistachio nuts

For the pistachio ice cream:
680g whipping cream
490g milk
90g glucose
8 eggs
300g caster sugar
200g pistachio paste
8g silk gel

For the pistachio baklava nest:
200g water
200g caster sugar
200g runny clear honey
Zest of 1 orange
Zest of 1 lemon
1 packet filo pastry
250g pistachio nuts
250g butter, melted

To serve:
3 moulds or containers such as ramekins measuring 100 fl oz

Method

For the honeycomb, line a tray with parchment paper. In a deep pan, melt the sugar, honey, glucose and water together on a gentle heat. When the sugar has melted, turn up the heat and simmer until a light amber coloured caramel forms. Whisk in the bicarbonate of soda until the mixture bubbles and increases in size. Pour the mixture into the lined tray. Be very careful as the mixture is very hot. Set aside to cool.

For the honeycomb mousse, whisk 250g of the whipping cream to form soft peaks, then set aside. In a separate mixing bowl, whisk the egg yolks with the sugar until thick, white and fluffy. Take the remaining 50g whipping cream and heat in a small pan over a gentle heat. Remove the gelatine from the cold water and add to the warm cream. Fold the whipped cream into the egg yolks. Crush the honeycomb into small pieces and fold into the mousse mixture. Ripple the honey into the mousse and pour into a 100 fl oz mould of your choice. Allow to set for 2 hours.

For the chocolate soil, line a tray with parchment paper and preheat the oven to 160°C (fan 140°C). Rub all of the ingredients together in a mixing bowl until a crumble has formed. Pour the mixture onto the lined tray and bake in the oven for 15-20 minutes. Blitz the mixture in a food processor until a fine dust forms. Set aside.

For the loukoumades, sift the flour and salt into a large mixing bowl, add the fresh yeast, honey and warm water. Mix until well combined. Cover with a damp cloth and prove for 40 minutes in a warm, dry place. Pour into a piping bag and pipe a teaspoonful of the mixture into a deep fat fryer. Fry for 3-4 minutes. Remove from the hot oil to a cloth and dust with ground cinnamon.

For the loukoumades sauce, add all of the ingredients to a pan and warm on a low heat until the sugar and butter have melted and dissolved. Pour over the fried loukoumades.

For the pistachio paste, heat the sugar and water together until the sugar has dissolved. Add the pistachio nuts and boil until the nuts soften. Place into a food processor and blitz to a smooth paste.

For the pistachio ice cream, heat the whipping cream, milk and glucose together in a pan on a low heat until boiling, then take off the heat. Whisk the eggs and caster sugar until mixed completely and pour into the boiled cream mixture. Mix in the pistachio paste and transfer to a clean saucepan. Return to a low heat and bring the mixture to 80°C, stirring constantly, then add the silk gel, remove from the heat and pass through a fine sieve. Leave to cool before churning the mixture in an ice cream machine.

For the pistachio baklava nest, preheat the oven to 180°C (fan 160°C). Place the water, sugar and honey in a small pan and bring to the boil. Stir until the sugar has dissolved and reduce the heat to let the syrup mixture simmer gently for 5 minutes. Add the zest from the orange and lemon and remove from the heat. Leave to cool down. Blitz the pistachio nuts until coarse. Take a layer of filo pastry and brush with melted butter and dust with the pistachio nuts. Repeat this 6 times until the base of the baklava is completed. Cut the baklava base to 1 inch squares.

Roll the remaining filo pastry into a Swiss roll shape and slice very finely. Dip into the melted butter, wrap the pastry around your finger and place on top of the baklava base. Fill the centre of the baklava nest with the blitzed pistachio nuts. Bake in the oven for 12-15 minutes or until golden brown. Remove from the oven and soak in the sugar and honey syrup.

Scatter the chocolate soil on your plate as pictured, place the fried loukamoudes into the centre of your first mould and add the pistachio baklava nest into a separate mould as shown. Add a dusting of chocolate soil over the top of the set honeycomb mousse in the third mould. Add a scoop of pistachio ice cream to finish.

Second Floor Bar
GARDEN OF EDEN

By mixing the cucumber within the drink, the vegetal notes of the Green Chartreuse are accentuated by the floral notes of elderflower. Serves 1.

Ingredients

40ml Portobello Road

10ml Green Chartreuse

25ml elderflower cordial

25ml lemon juice

1 egg white

Ice cubes

50ml strawberry lemonade

Dehydrated lemon slice

Cucumber, cut into ribbons

Strawberry, sliced

Method

Add the Portobello Road, Green Chartreuse, elderflower cordial, lemon juice and egg white into a shaker. Dry shake vigorously to emulsify the egg white into a foamy mixture, then add the ice and shake the mixture until mixed thoroughly.

Double-strain the liquid into a tall glass through a cocktail mesh strainer and slowly top off with the strawberry lemonade.

Garnish with a dehydrated lemon slice, cucumber ribbons and sliced strawberry.

Second Floor Bar
CONQUISTADOR

The natural sugars of the cherry and pectin give the drink a rich mouth-feel.
Serves 1.

Ingredients

40ml El Dorado 5 Year

10ml fig liqueur

10ml plum liqueur

1tsp Morello cherry jam

2 dashes of chocolate bitters

25ml lemon juice

1 fig

Ice cubes

Balsamic glaze

Edible gold paint

Method

Add the El Dorado 5 Year, fig liqueur, plum liqueur, Morello cherry jam, chocolate bitters and lemon juice into a shaker and shake vigorously to break up the Morello Cherry jam.

Strain into a tumbler glass over ice. Glaze the fig with balsamic glaze and brush a swipe of edible gold paint over the fruit to decorate.

A taste of Spain in
SPINNINGFIELDS

Showcasing the best in Spanish gastronomy, Ibérica's stunning Spinningfields restaurant offers Manchester's discerning residents an original dining experience.

The clean and modern design of Spinningfields is the ideal setting for the glamorous new addition to the Ibérica family – its first restaurant outside of London. Divided into an array of light and airy spaces, the contemporary setting brings a taste of Madrid's terrace culture to Manchester along with highly celebrated Spanish cooking. It has been designed from scratch, integrating the stunning glass façade with traditional Spanish décor, carefully balancing the two elements to create the ultimate in modern Spanish dining.

The ground floor contains a large bar which acts as a focal point, a mezzanine floor with further seating set around a theatrical open kitchen and there are two terraces, one on each side of the main entrance, where you can take in the buzz of bustling Spinningfields and enjoy a taste of the European outdoor dining culture.

The unique menu has been created by Ibérica's world renowned Executive Head Chef Nacho Manzano, who currently has an impressive three Michelin stars to his name (two for his highly celebrated Casa Marcial and one for La Salgar in Asturias, Spain).

Thanks to such a highly acclaimed chef behind the scenes, as well as his right hand man, César Garcia, the menu is impressive to say the least. Manchester foodies are enjoying sampling the tapas selection, as well as some truly inspirational modern Spanish main dishes.

The commitment to authentic Spanish produce of the very highest standards runs throughout the restaurant, and this is due to the wonderful relationships that Ibérica has forged with producers across Spain. The wine list has also been carefully considered to ensure that there is always the perfect bottle of wine available to complement the food.

Having tasted the food, many guests choose to visit the delicatessen, located inside the restaurant, so that they can take home a taste of the authentic cuisine to their own kitchens. With more than twenty olive oils on offer and a large selection of cheese and cured meats to buy, people are now whipping up Spanish meals in their own homes across Manchester.

Iberica

TWICE-COOKED LAMB, MARINATED CHERRIES,

with green pea purée and confit Bierzo peppers.

This dish is a trip to the very essence of the Castilian flavours. It combines lamb, which is a favourite product in the heart of Spain, with the confit red peppers from El Bierzo in the north of the region. The cherry tomatoes, infused in herbs, sherry vinegar, olive oil, salt and sugar, add a classic "escabeche" Spanish taste. Allow the tomatoes to marinate for 24 hours to soften and become more flavourful. Serves 4-6

Ingredients

For the lamb:

2 lamb necks

500g onion, chopped

250g carrot, chopped

50g red pepper, chopped

15g garlic, chopped

2g rosemary, chopped

3g tarragon, chopped

2g thyme, chopped

300ml white wine

Olive oil, for cooking

Salt and black pepper

For the marinated cherry tomatoes:

250g cherry tomatoes

5g salt

10g sugar

2g rosemary, chopped

2g thyme, chopped

50ml olive oil

25ml sherry vinegar

For the pea purée:

500g peas

25g butter

For the confit Bierzo peppers:

20g garlic, sliced

300ml olive oil

400g Bierzo peppers

40g sugar

Method

Fry the lamb necks in a little olive oil in a pan until sealed all over, then remove from the pan and set aside. Add the vegetables to the pan and cook until golden. Add the lamb necks back in again, then add the white wine and cook to reduce it. Add the herbs, cover with water and cook until the lamb is tender and the meat is coming away from the bones. Remove the necks from the stock and take the meat off the bone. Strain the stock and keep the vegetables.

Mix the vegetables with the deboned lamb meat (roughly done, not shredded) and season it. Press it into a deep tray to make a mould and chill it. Once chilled, take out of the tray and cut into portions. Meanwhile, place the stock in a pan and reduce it to a sauce.

For the tomatoes, fry the them on a very high heat until the skins burst. Mix with the salt and sugar, then the herbs, olive oil and sherry vinegar. Leave to marinate. These should be served at room temperature.

For the pea purée, cook the peas in boiling water with salt, then blend them in a blender with the butter and season.

For the confit Bierzo peppers, shallow-fry the sliced garlic in the olive oil on a low heat, add the peppers and sugar and cook slowly until soft and sweet.

To serve, pan-fry the lamb portions in a non-stick frying pan until crispy. (Finish in the oven if needed.) Finish on the plate with the sauce, the hot confit bierzo peppers and marinated cherry tomatoes on top, and with warm green pea purée on the side.

The heart and soul of
SALFORD QUAYS

Putting fresh, local and seasonal ingredients at the core of the menu
has always set Lime apart from its competitors, and this commitment to quality
is still at the heart of the business today.

The only independently-owned business in Salford Quays, there is something special about this thriving bar and restaurant, which has stood the test of time since it first opened 13 years ago. Its enviable position, close to the famous Lowry Theatre, makes it a favourite venue for a cross-section of Manchester's vibrant community. From formal business meetings and media lunches to pre-theatre dinners and evening cocktails, the bustling restaurant is busy all day long.

Owner David Vanderhook opened the restaurant having worked as a private chef cooking for some of the world's most discerning diners. From the kitchens on the QE2 to the homes of King Hussein of Jordan and fashion designer Valentino, it's fair to say that when it comes to creating inspiring food, David knows a thing or two.

Today, David has stepped back to leave the cooking in the capable hands of Head Chef Paul Hardman, whose skill and creativity are showcased in the impressive menu. Using only the freshest and finest ingredients, Paul and his talented team cook everything from scratch using seasonal produce where available.

There is no doubt that the cooking is high-end with some classic British dishes featuring on the menu – think Rack of Welsh Lamb on a Shallot Tarte Tatin or Lincolnshire Asparagus with Poached Egg and Hollandaise Sauce – but the chefs are also highly inventive and they embrace flavour combinations from around the world, such as Courgette and Chicken Moussaka or Chargrilled Squid with Thai Dressing.

The bustling bar is a popular spot for cocktail-lovers, which is no surprise given the impressive work behind the bar from the enthusiastic mixologists. All-time favourites are shaken and stirred beside modern inventions, so there is always something original to try.

Lime
ROAST HAKE WITH CHICKPEAS AND CHORIZO

Rich and warming yet still fresh and light, hake loins are roasted
to perfection in this flavour-packed dish. Serves 4.

Ingredients

150ml olive oil

2 large shallots, finely diced

1 onion, finely diced

1 large carrot, finely diced

150g diced chorizo

1 tin chopped tomatoes

50ml vegetable stock

200g tinned chick peas (rinsed and drained)

½ bunch flat leaf parsley, roughly chopped

4 hake loins, 8oz each

half a lemon (or to taste)

Salt and freshly ground black pepper

Method

Preheat the oven to 220°C.

Place a heavy pan over a medium heat and, when hot, add 100ml of the olive oil, the shallots, onion and carrot. Fry for 3-4 minutes until softened.

Add the chorizo and allow to colour slightly.

Add the chopped tomatoes and bring to a simmer, then add the vegetable stock.

Cook for 15 minutes, stirring occasionally.

Add the chickpeas and allow to simmer for a further 5 minutes. Finally add the chopped parsley. Keep warm.

Rub and season the hake loins with the remaining 50ml of olive oil and place skin-side down in a hot ovenproof pan over a medium heat. Cook for 3 minutes and then transfer to the oven to roast for 5 minutes. Turn the hake loins over and place back in the oven for a further 3 minutes.

Pour the chickpea and chorizo mixture into a deep dish, place the hake loins on top, add a squeeze of lemon and serve.

We are totally MAD FOR IT

Landmarks of Manchester's social scene, Rosylee, Infamous Diner, The Fitzgerald and Walrus share one mission: to provide the best time possible for all their guests through great music, spaces, staff, drinks and food.

Where better to start a tour of the Northern Quarter than Stevenson Square and the stunning Rosylee with its huge outdoor terrace and gorgeous interior. Come rain or shine, the recently updated menu offers the best of classic British cuisine using locally sourced ingredients. Burgers and skewers cooked in the INKA charcoal oven are stars of the show – the chicken, duck, lamb and beef are sizzled to mouth-watering perfection in the 400°C oven. Comfy booths, hearty breakfasts, amazing drinks, friendly service, a glorious suntrap and table service, no wonder Rosylee is one of Manchester's event hot spots. It has played host to many a press launch, corporate event, fashion collection and product launch in the past.

Step across to the atmospheric drinking den that is The Fitzgerald. Vintage vibes, splendid décor and 1920's glamour sets this unique venue apart from its neighbours. It's a hidden spot in which to enjoy a delicious cocktail while local musicians perform live jazz and blues into the early hours – a corner of 1920's New York in the heart of Manchester. From cocktail tastings and mixology competitions to private afternoon teas and murder mystery dinners, this characterful space makes all kinds of events truly magical.

Next up on the Northern Quarter tour is Walrus, where the cocktails are still flowing but the menu also draws in the crowds. This is the venue for an after-work drink, to enjoy a cocktail before hitting the secret dance floor in the basement, or to relax with a beer in a large comfy booth while sharing a platter of snacks or tucking into a burger, pizza or portion of fish and chips. Reserve a booth for a group of friends or book the downstairs bar for a private party.

The Northern Quarter certainly has its drinking hotspots covered, but what about when you really want to focus on food? When only a classic American plate of hand-made deliciousness will do, Infamous Diner has it covered. Manchester's first independent all-American diner, the portions are big, the service is smiley and the atmosphere is everything you'd expect from its raspberry pink booths and silver ceilings. The true diner spirit includes free refills on filter coffee, authentic American breakfasts and some of the best hot dogs, burgers, fries and shakes this side of the Atlantic.

MAD Developments Ltd

Rosylee
BUBBLE AND SQUEAK POTATO CAKE WITH POACHED EGG AND BÉARNAISE

Classic British comfort food at its best. Serves 4.

Ingredients

800g potatoes

1 carrot

¼ small cabbage

5 leeks

¼ head of broccoli

400g spinach

2 eggs yolks

1 tsp white wine vinegar

160g melted unsalted butter

1 sprig of tarragon

100ml double cream

4 eggs

160ml extended life rapeseed oil

40g unsalted butter

Salt and pepper

Method

Separately peel and cut the potatoes and carrots into 2 cm dice. Remove the outer damaged cabbage and leek leaves and cut into 1cm slices. Cut the broccoli and wash the spinach.

Place the 2 egg yolks and vinegar in a metal bowl set over a pan of simmering hot water and whisk until it starts to thicken, but do not scramble the egg yolks. Slowly whisk the 160g melted butter into the thickened egg yolks one ladle at a time. If the béarnaise becomes too thick, then add a little water to thin down slightly. Add the seasoning to taste along with the chopped tarragon.

Place the diced potatoes and carrots in separate pans and cover with cold water and bring to the boil. Simmer until they are soft and drain separately in a colander over a sink. Boil the sliced cabbage, leeks and broccoli until tender. Drain the vegetables very well.

Mash the potato and add the double cream and seasoning. Combine the mashed potato and cooked vegetables and season to taste. Form four equal-sized 'cakes'.

Heat the oil in a shallow frying pan and fry until the cakes are golden and the core temperature is 75°C when probed for at least 2 minutes. Heat the butter in another shallow frying pan and add the washed spinach.

Poach the 4 eggs to your preference.

Assemble the cooked bubble and squeak cakes on a plate, topped with the cooked spinach, poached eggs and then spoon over the béarnaise sauce. Garnish with cracked black pepper.

The Fitzgerald
FRENCH MARTINILLA

Ingredients

2 blackberries

2 raspberries

5ml Monin vanilla syrup or homemade vanilla syrup

32.5ml Cariel vanilla vodka

12.5ml Chambord black raspberry liqueur

50ml freshly squeezed pineapple juice

Raspberry and blackberry, to garnish

Method

Start by muddling the berries together using a muddler or the end of a rolling pin in a cocktail shaker/ Boston glass. Add the vanilla syrup to the berries and combine to create a purée. To this purée add the vodka, Chambord and pineapple juice. Fill the rest of the glass with cubes of ice, add the lid of your cocktail shaker and shake really hard really quickly for at least 15 seconds. Using a cocktail strainer (tea strainer will do if you do not have one) strain into a chilled coupé or martini glass, making sure you keep a nice froth on top. Garnish with a raspberry and blackberry and serve!

Infamous Diner
CORN DOGS

You can't beat this classic American snack. Makes 4.

Ingredients

220g polenta cornmeal

60g plain flour

2 level tsp cornflour

Maldon sea salt, to taste

Cracked black pepper, to taste

1 level tsp baking powder

Pinch of bicarbonate of soda

½ tsp cayenne pepper

2 large white onions

3-4 sliced green jalapeños

20g sweetcorn niblets

125ml buttermilk

200ml whole milk

4 pork and beef frankfurters

Method

In a medium mixing bowl, combine the polenta, plain flour, cornflour, salt, pepper, baking powder, bicarbonate of soda and cayenne pepper.

Peel and dice the onion and jalapeños and, in a separate bowl, combine the onions, jalapeños, corn, buttermilk and milk. Add the dry ingredients to the wet ingredients all at once, and stir only enough times to bring the batter together; there should be lumps. Set the batter aside and allow to rest for 10 minutes.

Preheat the deep fat fryer to 180°C. Transfer enough batter to almost fill a large drinking glass. Refill the glass as needed. Place each hot dog on a stick, and quickly dip in and out of the batter. Immediately and carefully place each hot dog into the oil, and cook until the coating is golden brown; about 4-5 minutes. With tongs, remove to a cooling rack and allow to drain for 3-5 minutes. Serve with American-style mustard, ketchup or sweet chilli sauce.

Infamous Diner
BUTTERMILK PANCAKES WITH BLUEBERRIES

A favourite breakfast dish on the Infamous Diner menu. Makes 12.

Ingredients

125g wild blueberries

25g caster sugar

175g self-raising flour

3 pinches of salt

1 tsp bicarbonate of soda (heaped)

100ml buttermilk

250ml semi-skimmed milk

1 egg

50g unsalted butter, melted

Butter, for frying

Method

Place the blueberries and half of the caster sugar in a microwavable container and heat in the microwave for 2 minutes. Stir and then give it another 2 minutes.

In a clean bowl sift the self-raising flour, salt, remaining caster sugar and the bicarbonate of soda. In a separate bowl or jug, mix together the buttermilk, milk, egg and melted butter. Pour the wet mixture into the dry ingredients and stir to combine. Do not over beat – if the batter is lumpy, set it aside for a few minutes and any lumps will disappear.

Melt a small knob of butter in a large frying pan. Using a ladle, pour some batter into the pan to make a pancake. Depending on the size of your pan, you may be able to make more than one pancake at a time, or if you are confident you can use two pans at the same time. Cook the pancakes for about a minute, or until the underside is golden-brown and the top is bubbling. Then turn them over using a palette knife or fish slice and cook for another minute. Keep the pancakes warm in a very low oven while you cook the remaining batter. Serve the pancakes stacked on top of each other, topped with the blueberries.

Walrus
BBQ CHICKEN WINGS

Sticky and delicious finger food, perfect for sharing. Serves 4.

Ingredients

1 white onion

1 clove garlic

Splash of cold-pressed rapeseed oil

110g tomato sauce

½ teaspoon cayenne pepper

200g tinned chopped tomatoes

50g dark brown soft sugar

1 tbsp Worcestershire sauce

2 tbsp red wine vinegar

½ teaspoon smoked paprika

1kg 2-bone chicken wings

Method

Peel the white onion and garlic. Put the onion and garlic in a food processor and blend. Heat the oil in a heavy based saucepan over a medium-high heat. Add the puréed onion and garlic and cook, stirring frequently, until it starts to brown. Add the tomato sauce, cayenne pepper, chopped tomatoes, dark brown sugar, Worcestershire sauce, red wine vinegar and smoked paprika and bring to a simmer. Simmer for about 45 minutes, stirring frequently. Once the sauce has darkened and thickened, remove it from the heat.

Preheat the oven to 180°C. Combine the chicken wings with the BBQ sauce and roast the wings in the oven for approximately 40 minutes, until the chicken wings are cooked. Serve with extra BBQ sauce and some celery sticks.

Walrus
SOLERO

Ingredients

37.5ml passionfruit vodka

12.5ml passionfruit syrup

20ml vanilla syrup

Half a lemon

2 teaspoons of sugar

Lemonade

Ripe mango

To garnish

Cherry

Lemon slice

Orange slice

Method

For the mango puree

To make the mango puree, peel and pit the mango and put it in a food processor with a couple of teaspoons of sugar and the juice of a quarter of a lemon. Run until smooth and keep refrigerated for up to 3 days (this is also delicious in smoothies or drizzled over ice cream).

For the Cocktail

Measure out 25ml of mango puree and add to the cocktail shaker, along with the passionfruit vodka, passionfruit syrup and vanilla syrup. (If you do not have passionfruit syrup you can add half a fresh passionfruit, and increase the vanilla syrup to 25ml).

Squeeze the remaining quarter of the lemon into the shaker. Add ice and shake vigorously.

Strain using cocktail strainer and pour into a hurricane or sling glass full of cubed ice. Top up with lemonade, drizzle a little of the mango puree and garnish with a cherry, slice of lemon and slice of orange. Enjoy!

Award-Winning
PIES & TARTS

Mother-daughter team, The Manchester Tart Company have put local regional recipes back on the menu in Manchester, much to the delight of local food-lovers.

A natural talent for baking runs in the blood for Clare Hillyer and her mum Ann Taylor. For Clare, a life-long love of cooking was inspired by and inherited from her mother, who worked as a professional chef-lecturer for over 20 years. Throughout her career, which involved training chefs for the industry, Ann became qualified to the highest levels and developed a great interest in the history of baking and cooking.

It was Clare's wedding that inspired the creation of their family business. Trying to find someone to make authentic and traditional Manchester tarts for her wedding day was proving impossible, so Clare and her mum set about making their own. They were so successful on the big day, that Clare was inspired to embark on an exciting venture with her mum to continue making their delicious tarts.

The business is centred on local classics – some are much-loved recipes that have stood the test of time, such as Eccles cakes and Manchester tarts of course, along with a whole host of heritage recipes that they have brought back into the hearts and mouths of their customers, such as Lancashire foot and Bury black pudding tarts.

Clare and Ann are continually researching traditional recipes, at the same time keeping up to date with contemporary trends, developing innovative recipes of their own using the very finest local ingredients. The process of making the pies and tarts is very labour-intensive, as everything is hand-made from scratch with no corners being cut. But that's the only way to achieve the very best results, insists Clare, and it's what they believe has made their small business stand out.

The successes speak for themselves – they've won gold stars at the Great Taste awards for their products every year since 2010, and 2015 has seen the addition of 2 gold stars for their shin of beef and ox kidney pie and previously an impressive 3 gold stars for the Cumberland mutton pie.

What is amazing about these top-quality products, which are supplied to some of Manchester's finest delis and cafés, as well as being sold at markets and online, is that they are all produced in Clare's large home kitchen in South Manchester. It's an environment where their harmonious working relationship thrives and the very highest professional standards are achieved – it's no wonder the orders are coming in as quickly as the awards!

Photos: Jon Hülyer

Another LEVEL

One of Manchester's most iconic restaurants, Aiden Byrne's critically acclaimed Manchester House is one of the jewels in the city's culinary crown.

Opened in 2013 and set within an unassuming office block in Spinningfields, Manchester House is home to the highly celebrated Chef Aiden Byrne, who has risen from a humble Merseyside background to become known as one of Britain's most adventurous and creative cooks.

First impressions are taken seriously by the front of house staff who endeavour to achieve the highest quality service without the pressure that can so often be associated with fine dining restaurants. The focus at Manchester House is "fine, fun, funky", so guests can expect to enjoy seriously good food in a more relaxed and fun setting, perfectly suited to its Spinningfields home.

"It's all about eating well, trying new things and enjoying a bit of what they like", for Aiden Byrne – and what's not to love about that? There are certainly plenty of new things to try on the menu, with some classic ingredients sitting beside intriguing offerings. We're talking about inspiring combinations like Rioja-braised Aylesbury snails, razor clams, Baby Gem and Stilton or veal fillet and sweetbread with lobster and Braeburn apple.

From the reasonably priced lunch menu to the extravagant 15-course tasting menu, this is a venue where foodies can experience a taste of modern culinary creativity that stands out from the usual fine dining fare. Inventive twists and ingenious presentation complement the delicate balance of flavours from the carefully sourced ingredients. Vegetarians are suitably catered for with a complete vegetarian tasting menu and à la carte menu available – mouthwatering dishes such as warm Ribblesdale cheese and onion soup or truffle pappardelle with cauliflower and truffle couscous are much more than meat-free afterthoughts.

The wine list is impressive, but there is also a wide choice of red, white, rosé and sparkling wine served by the glass, too. In fact, guests are welcome to come simply for a drink in the bar – another aspect which makes this restaurant genuinely welcoming, as Aiden explains, "so you can pop in whenever you're in town, whether you want to eat or not".

Photo: James Brown www.jamesbrownphotographer.co.uk

Manchester House

HAY-BAKED MALLARD

with blood sausage purée, fermented beetroot and lingonberries.

Ingredients

2 whole mallards that have been plucked and cleaned (retain the liver and heart)

2kg baby beetroot

100g fine sea salt

100g honey

25g lingonberries

150g uncooked black pudding (diced into small pieces)

250g duck fat

2 good handfuls of heather

3 good handfuls of fresh straw

5 sprigs of fresh thyme

10g sherry vinegar

Method

Trim and clean the baby beets, cut them in half lengthways and place in a sealable parfait jar with the fine sea salt, the honey and water.

Seal the lid and leave for ten days, allowing the honey and the water to ferment.

Drain the fermenting liquor from the beets and set aside, pat the beets dry and place on a bed of heather, wrap in tin foil and bake in an oven at 140°C for 45 minutes, leave wrapped up until cooled and required.

Reduce the fermenting liquor by three quarters and place into a blender, whilst it is rotating gradually add the black pudding and blend until smooth, pass through a fine sieve and set aside.

Warm the duck fat up gently to 80°C and pop in the duck hearts and cook at this temperature for 4 hours, keep warm.

In a large hot cast iron casserole pan that has a sealable lid seal the well seasoned mallards all around (you are looking for a deep caramelisation) place the caramelised birds somewhere warm (so they don't cool down) and clean the pan of any dirty fat oil, try your hardest to keep the pan warm too.

Place 50% of the hay, thyme and heather in the base of the warm pan, sit the birds on top and then completely cover them with the remaining 50%. Place a digital probe into the cavity of the bird and place the lid on top, ensure it is fully sealed.

Once the bird has reached 50°C then remove from the pot. This will usually take an hour depending on the size of the bird.

In a small, hot, non-stick frying pan with a dash of oil add the seasoned livers along with the lingonberries and sauté very quickly, no longer then 30 seconds, de-glaze the pan with the sherry vinegar and set aside.

When the bird is cooked, carve away the breasts and place onto 4 warm plates, spoon the blood puree next to the breast and arrange the baked, fermented beetroot alongside them. Add the livers, the lingonberries and the confit heart and serve.

Meet and Eat at THE MET

The Metropolitan combines modern menus, fine drinks and relaxing vibes, all housed within a grand Victorian building in the heart of West Didsbury.

The leafy south Manchester suburb of West Didsbury is home to the beautiful old railway hotel, which was lovingly transformed into The Metropolitan in 1998. The character of the Victorian building has been retained throughout and its historic charm is evident from the homely library with its real log fires and book-lined walls to the light and airy conservatory restaurant furnished with antique tables and chairs.

Like any good pub, one of the things that makes The Metropolitan so special is its commitment to its customers. From business lunches and afternoon teas to family weekend gatherings and friends enjoying a Saturday night out, loyal regulars are at the heart and soul of this local gem. People who used to spend their Saturday evenings here 17 years ago are now bringing their children in on Sunday afternoons – and many of the dedicated staff have been working here throughout that time, too. Being listed within the top 60 hospitality employers by The Caterer is testament to the incredible team atmosphere that permeates the bar, kitchen, restaurant and office here.

Famous locally for its drinks menu, The Metropolitan is home to real ales, continental beers, malt whiskies and fine wines, which have all been carefully selected to complement the exceptional food on offer.

The menu has a British feel, with some much-loved Met classics and plenty of quirky modern twists. The famous Metropolitan burger has been on the menu since the year it opened and is just as popular with the regulars today as it was then! Although there are those firm favourites that they wouldn't dare remove, the chefs rely on using local produce wherever possible, so the menus change with the seasons, too, meaning there are always fresh and innovative things to try.

Local suppliers include W.H. Frost Butchers in Chorlton, family-run Cheshire Wholesale and Easy Fish in Heaton Moor. Many of the incredible cakes are made by local foodies, such as Silver Apples and Black Cake Bakery (who create the delicious vegan cakes). Supporting other local businesses and charities underpins the community-based ethos of this renowned establishment, so it's no wonder they were rewarded with a Heroes in the Community Award. With such enthusiastic teamwork at all levels, this West Didsbury favourite looks set to see many more successes in years to come.

The Metropolitan
SEA BASS WITH CHICKPEA

and sweet potato curry, onion bhaji bon bons and mint yoghurt

Warming curry, crisp bhaji bonbons and fresh minty yoghurt provide the
perfect backdrop for a light and fresh sea bass fillet. Serves 1.

Ingredients

For the curry:

1 large sweet potato

15ml rapeseed oil

1 red onion

5g cumin

5g ground coriander

3g turmeric

100g chickpeas

250g chopped tomato

For the bhaji bon bons:

1 white onion

5g turmeric

15g freshly chopped coriander

10g plain flour

Salt and pepper

For the dressing:

10g Greek yoghurt

5g freshly chopped mint

5g diced cucumber

For the sea bass:

10ml rapeseed oil

5g butter

1 large sea bass fillet

3g Maldon sea salt, to season

Method

For the curry, preheat the oven to 180°C. Peel and chop the sweet potato, place on a baking tray, drizzle over the oil and roast in the preheated oven for 15 minutes until soft.

Slice the red onion and sweat off with the spice mix until soft, then add the chickpeas and chopped tomato and cook for 25 minutes on a moderate heat. Season to taste.

Add the sweet potato at the end of the cooking process, as you want the curry to be chunky in consistency

For the bhajis, sweat the white onion off until translucent, add the turmeric and cook the spice so that it's not grainy. Add salt and pepper and the fresh chopped coriander. To make the bhajis, mix with the flour and roll into small bon bons. Shallow-fry until golden.

Mix the dressing ingredients together.

For the sea bass, heat the rapeseed oil and butter in a non-stick pan and pan-fry the sea bass fillet, skin-side down, until crispy, and then turn onto the flesh side to finish off the cooking process.

Assemble as per the photograph – for a decadent touch, you can use micro herbs to decorate the dish.

All Set to
MIX THINGS UP

British cooking, global flavours and local produce – Mish Mash's unmistakeable medley of fun, flavour and flair has seen it establish itself firmly in the hearts of Chorlton locals.

Located on Beech Road, this stunning eatery is turning heads and wowing food-lovers with its eye-catching style and impressive cooking. It is the culmination of years of hard work by owner James Plant, whose impressive 25 years' experience in the food industry has led him to opening this exciting venture.

James, who has worked in top-end establishments for much of his career, wanted to put the focus of Mish Mash firmly on fun and flavour. He hails from a family of foodies and celebrates a natural approach to cooking where both he and his chefs can let their personalities shine. This commitment is clear in the simple and carefully considered menu, which encompasses a few classics with quirky twists and some great blackboard specials, including exciting vegetarian options.

Keeping the menu fairly short enables James and his team to focus on being creative and having fun with ingredients, capturing the best each season has to offer and exploring the amazing produce available in Manchester. Take a look at the specials board for a glimpse into the creative freedom that Mish Mash encourages in its chefs – fantastic for the regulars who know there will always be something new and exciting to try.

The focus on flavour doesn't end with the food. Whether it's selecting the wine list or developing the cocktail menu, James has taken the time to put taste and creativity at the heart of everything – some of the signature cocktails have been honed for years before appearing on his bar menu.

From the urban art and graffiti by local artists that adorn the walls to the eclectic music, the ambience of Mish Mash is perfectly designed to show off the philosophy of playfulness and adventure. With such creativity at its core, it's impossible not to be wowed by this eatery on each and every visit.

Mish Mash
MOJITO CHICKEN

with wild rice, jalapeño salsa, roasted peppers and flatbread

This zesty, minty chicken with its unusual rum-based marinade is packed full of flavour. It's best if left to marinate for 12-36 hours, so you'll need to start preparing this at least a day in advance. Serves 2.

Ingredients

4 boneless, skinless chicken thighs, chopped into bite-sized chunks

100g wild rice

1 red pepper

1 tbsp golden/Demerara sugar

25ml golden rum, such as Mount Gay or Cockspur

Juice of ½ lime

4 mint leaves, chopped

1 flatbread, cut in half

Lime wedges and mint sprig tips, to garnish

For the marinade:

1 lime

25ml golden rum, such as Mount Gay or Cockspur

A whole sprig of mint leaves (about 5g), torn

1 tbsp golden/Demerara sugar

2 tsp olive oil

Salt and black pepper

For the jalapeño salsa:

½ red onion, finely chopped

1 clove garlic, finely chopped

Fresh jalapeño, chopped, to taste (we use ½ chilli, deseeded)

6 baby plum tomatoes, blanched, peeled and chopped

2 tsp lemon juice

1 tbsp olive oil

Salt and black pepper

Method

Start by making the marinade. Grate the zest of the lime into a bowl. Slice the zested lime in half and thoroughly squeeze all the juice into the bowl. Trim the flesh to add in too. Add the remaining marinade ingredients and stir together, then add the chopped chicken thighs and mix in well. Cover and place in the fridge to marinate for a minimum 12 hours and a maximum of 36 hours.

For the salsa, with a small frying pan on medium heat, lightly fry the onion, then add the garlic and then the jalapeño and fry off. Add the chopped tomato, lemon juice, olive oil and seasoning and cook to reduce by half.

When ready to cook, preheat the oven to 180°C.

Bring a pan of water to the boil, add the wild rice and cook following the packet instructions (usually about 25 minutes).

Slice the peppers to create large sides. Place in a baking tray, drizzle over a little olive oil and sprinkle with salt and pepper. Roast in the preheated oven for 20 minutes.

Bring a suitable pan to a medium heat and add the golden/Demerara sugar to begin caramelising. Lift the chicken from the marinade, keeping the marinade, and add to the pan (you may get some flames). Toss around to sear all sides. Once the meat is sealed, add the rum into the hot pan to flambé the chicken (see note). Add the remaining marinade (which may again catch fire) and cook, stirring, for 10 minutes or until the chicken is cooked. Squeeze in the lime juice and chopped mint leaves.

To serve, place the drained wild rice on the plate, with the roasted peppers, mojito chicken and salsa on top, and finish each portion with half a flatbread, rolled up. The dominant flavours should be mint and lime – so we find the best garnish to be the tip of the mint sprig and a lime wedge.

Note on flambéing

This will cause relatively high flames, but don't be too scared. It may light immediately, or it may need the pan tilting to catch the heat on the gas at the side of the pan. Alternatively, if using convection hobs, a lighter can be used to set the alcohol on fire. When flambéing, move the pan occasionally to prevent sticking.

Stay True to YOUR ROOTS

With the success of his critically acclaimed restaurant The French leading the way in the Manchester fine-dining scene, Simon Rogan opened a second, more informal brasserie-style establishment at the Midland hotel. Welcome to Mr. Cooper's House & Garden.

Simon Rogan is widely known for producing some of the UK's most original and inspirational menus in his critically acclaimed restaurants, which include the two-Michelin star L'Enclume in Cumbria and highly celebrated Manchester favourite, The French. He also launched Fera at Claridge's in London's Mayfair in Spring 2014. With Mr. Cooper's House & Garden, Simon is focusing his culinary style on creative cooking and international flavours within a beautifully designed library and garden ambience.

Housed within the grand architecture of the Midland Hotel, this magnificent restaurant celebrates the heritage of Mr. Cooper's house and his famous gardens, which sat on the site in 1819, while offering a unique, creative and contemporary dining experience.

The dining settings are as diverse as the menus. Opt to sit in the garden by the towering tree with the cascading wall of plants providing the ultimate backdrop to a special meal, enjoy drinks in the library or find a cosy spot in the study in one of the leather booths.

When it comes to selecting your meal, the choices cover favourites from around the world – classic combinations which have been given deliciously different twists by Simon Rogan's unparalleled culinary skills and some unique offerings that will amaze and inspire. From raw beef with paw paw, tomato jam and rye to Stichelton, red cabbage, coleslaw, mustard and salted walnuts, the starters offer a glimpse into the remarkable taste combinations being put together here. For main course, the very finest fish, meat and vegetables are transformed into modern show-stoppers – think grilled bream, caramelised calamari, chickpeas and hazelnuts or Cumbrian rib steak, truffle pudding and purple potato latke.

The dessert list continues the creative masterclass in bringing together unusual ingredients to create incredible flavour combinations, with pineapple tarte tatin, spiced ice cream and pepper caramel or macerated plums, buttermilk custard, flapjack and sorrel featuring on the jaw-dropping menu.

In addition to a fixed-price early-evening house menu, ideal for pre-theatre, there is also a great-value midweek lunch menu and a mouth-watering Sunday roast menu, providing options for all occasions, allowing everyone to enjoy a taste of Simon Rogan's gastronomic flair in these truly sensational surroundings at Mr. Cooper's House & Garden.

Mr Cooper's
SAGE-CRUSTED PORK CHOP

tofu green beans, creamed potatoes and pork sauce

This stunning dish from Mr. Cooper's House & Garden by Simon Rogan
requires a few stages of preparation, but most of it can be prepared in advance
and put together easily to serve. Serves 4.

Ingredients

4 thick pork chops

Maldon sea salt

20g parsley, finely chopped

Sunflower oil, for frying

For the sage crust:

11 slices of sliced white bread, crusts removed

15 sage leaves

40g Parmesan, finely grated

1 egg yolk

200g unsalted butter

15ml double cream

5g fine salt

For the tofu green beans:

600g silken tofu

10g light soy sauce

10g sake

90g toasted sesame seeds

60g caster sugar

5g fine salt

400g blanched green beans

For the pork sauce:

1kg chopped pork bones

1kg minced pork

6 carrots, peeled and sliced

6 banana shallots, peeled and sliced

4 garlic cloves

10 thyme sprigs

2 bay leaves

600ml dry white wine

3 litres white chicken stock

For the creamed potatoes:

500g Maris Piper potatoes, peeled and chopped

250g unsalted butter

50ml whole milk

Fine salt, to taste

Method

For the sage crust, mix all the ingredients together and blitz in a food blender. Roll between two sheets of silicone paper and leave in the fridge to go hard. Then cut into squares and leave in the fridge until needed.

For the tofu dressing for the green beans, blitz the silken tofu, light soy sauce, sake, toasted sesame seeds, caster sugar and salt together in a food blender, pass through a sieve and check the seasoning. Keep in the fridge along with the blanched beans until needed.

For the pork sauce, preheat the oven to 180°C. Roast the pork bones and pork mince separately in the preheated oven until golden. Then pass off the fat. Next, in a large pan, cook the vegetables along with the thyme and bay leaves until they go golden. Deglaze with the white wine, then add the roasted bones and mince. Cover with the white chicken stock. Bring to the boil and simmer for 2½ hours. Pass through a fine sieve and cook until reduced to a sauce consistency.

Meanwhile, for the creamed potatoes, cook the chopped potatoes in salted boiling water until cooked, then pass through a fine sieve and add the butter and milk. Check the seasoning. Keep warm while you assemble the dish.

Add a small amount of sunflower oil to a non-stick pan. Once hot, season the pork chops with Maldon sea salt, add to the pan and colour both sides. Allow to rest for 5 minutes. Coat the chops in the sage crust and cook under the grill until golden.

Heat the creamed potatoes up, if necessary, as well as the green beans in the tofu dressing. Place one large spoonful of creamed potatoes onto each plate, add the green beans in tofu dressing and finish with a pork chop. Heat up the pork sauce, if necessary, and spoon around the dish. Finish with chopped parsley.

Palate PLEASERS

Welcome to Palate, the Chorlton wine bar where the accompanying food is taken as seriously as the vintage.

In the bustling neighbourhood of Chorlton, Palate offers something unique to the local food and drink scene. Owners Jamie Langrish and Jonny Booth wanted to create a space where good-quality wine was the order of the day, without all the pressure that is often associated with wine bars. Their aim was to build a fantastic wine list and make it accessible to people who, like them, simply love a nice glass of wine.

The warm and welcoming atmosphere shows that they have succeeded in their aim of breaking down those wine bar barriers. The wine list hangs on the wall and, although there are 80 carefully chosen bottles on offer, there is no sommelier to cast disapproving glances, no pressure to select the appropriate colour and certainly no judgements from the friendly staff. Of course if you do want some advice, they are more than happy to make recommendations.

The menu is varied and inspiring. As the wines are taken from all around the world, the food has international twists too. The talented chef takes inspiration from the wines to create dishes that work well with their favourite bottles. There is a focus on food for sharing here – just as you share a bottle of wine. This is a place where couples and groups are encouraged to enjoy the simple pleasure of shared eating – maybe start with a charcuterie board, followed by a main course to share and then perhaps linger over the cheese platter.

Although there are many spices and flavours from around the world, the ingredients are all free-range and sourced as locally as possible. The charcuterie and cheese platters are British (the cheeses are all from Neal's Yard in London), and the Suffolk chorizo and air-dried venison carpaccio certainly make a refreshing change from the usual offerings from our Italian and French neighbours.

Palate
HOT CORONATION CHICKEN

Full of flavour, this British classic just needs the perfect glass of wine
to accompany it. Serves 1.

Ingredients

1 tsp olive oil

1 tsp butter

1 small garlic clove

A squeeze of lime juice

285g French-trimmed skin-on chicken breast

85g basmati rice

1 tsp coriander

1 tsp ghee

½ tsp mild curry powder

100ml chicken stock

1 tbsp good-quality mango chutney

100ml double cream

30g mange tout

Sultanas and small handful of watercress to garnish

Method

Preheat the oven to 190°C. Heat the oil and butter in an ovenproof pan, turn the heat down, add the garlic and lime juice and cook for 30 seconds. Place the chicken in the pan, skin-side down, and cook until lightly browned and then seal all over. Transfer the chicken to the oven and cook for 18 minutes.

While the chicken is in the oven, rinse the rice thoroughly with cold water and place in a small pan with 1.5 to 1.75 times the water to rice. Salt the rice and water and place over a high heat. Once the water begins to boil, turn the heat to low and place a lid on the pan. Continue to cook until the water has been absorbed (around 10 minutes). Turn off the heat and allow the rice to rest while you make the sauce and the chicken finishes. Separate the rice grains with a fork and add the coriander just before plating.

Melt the ghee in a hot pan and add the curry powder. Cook the curry powder in the ghee for 1 minute to bloom the spices (be careful not to burn) and add the chicken stock. Bring the stock and spice mixture to a simmer and melt in the mango chutney. Turn down the heat and stir in the double cream. Continue to cook until the sauce thickens enough to coat the back of a spoon.

While the sauce thickens, quickly simmer the mange tout for 2 minutes.

Make a timbale with the coriander rice, stack the mange tout beside it and rest the chicken against them. Pour over the sauce, scatter over the sultanas and place the watercress on top to finish.

The spirit of CHORLTON

In a leafy south Manchester suburb, The Parlour embodies everything that is important to a proper pub – great home-cooked food, local beers on tap and a sense of community spirit.

When Rupert Hill, Jonny Booth and Jamie Langrish opened The Parlour in 2010, they had a clear vision in mind. They wanted to create a pub with real heart and soul, where people are greeted like old friends, the atmosphere is warm, the drinks selection is exciting and the food is cooked from scratch. And it's fair to say they have achieved just that in The Parlour.

It was always intended to be a food-driven pub, but the team at The Parlour go above and beyond the usual nod to local suppliers and fresh ingredients. The meat comes from neighbouring W.H. Frost Butchers and they whole-heartedly support the Manchester Veg People, which started in 2009 as an informal group of organic growers and is now an established co-operative of growers and buyers who supply locally grown food to businesses. As the vegetables that arrive on their doorstep vary depending on what delights are being harvested from the local allotments, their menu also changes

with it. This is seasonal cooking in its truest sense.

The Sunday roast was named Best Sunday Roast by the Observer in 2012 and has featured among the runners up every year since – no wonder it has people queuing up outside for it each week!

True to its proper pub vibe, the beer selection is exciting and varied with hand-picked cask ales from local brewers such as Robinsons from Stockport and Redwillow from Macclesfield, as well as interesting small producers from around the world. With its cosy corners and comfy sofas, there is no better place to enjoy a friendly pint with family and friends. In fact whether it's dinner and a glass of wine, an after-work drink or a lazy weekend afternoon, there is always a warm welcome at The Parlour.

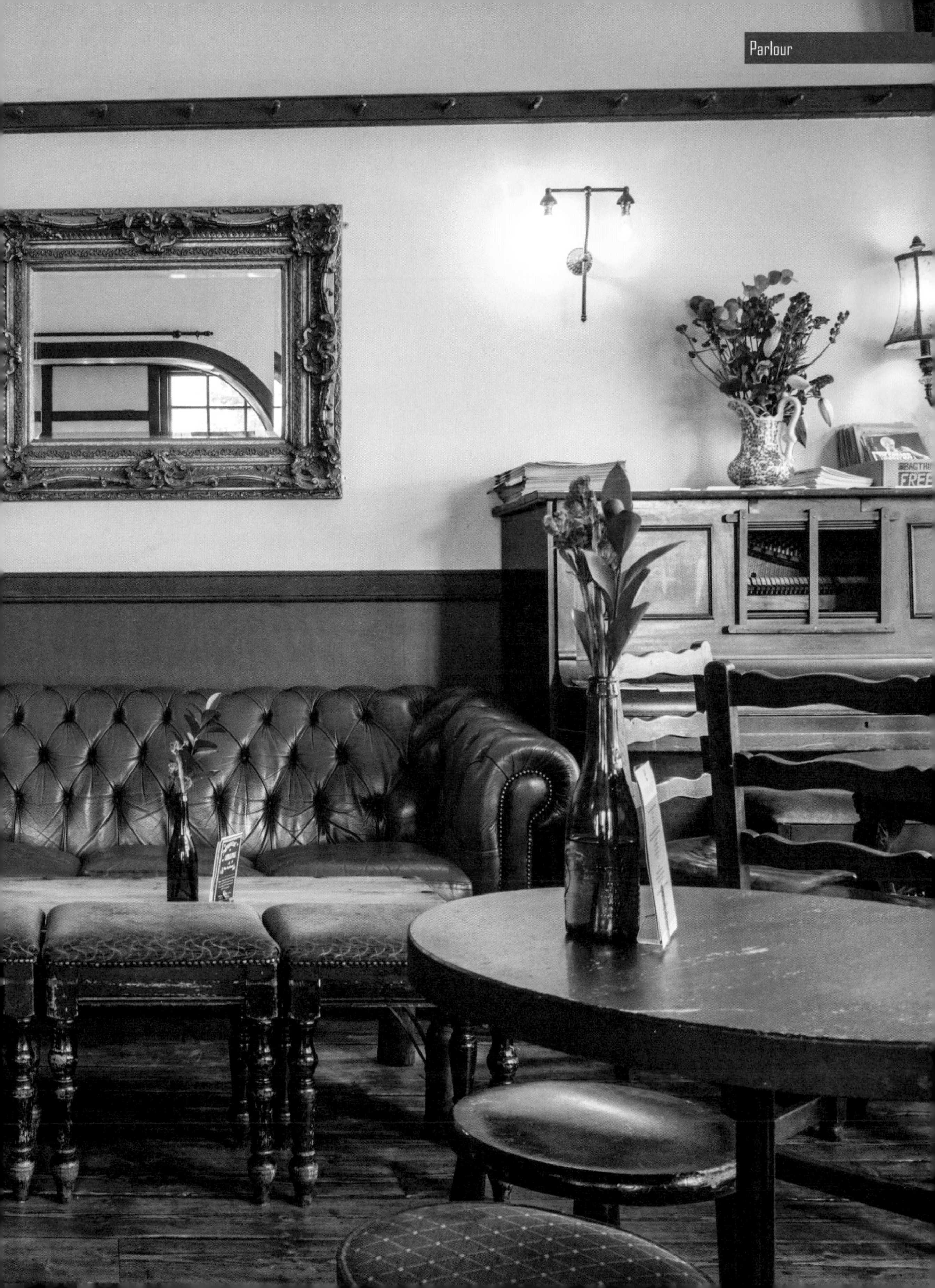

The Parlour
CHESHIRE OX CHEEK SLOW-BRAISED
in Robinson's Old Tom Dark Ale with celeriac mash, roasted turnips and horseradish and thyme dumplings.

Warming comfort food using the best of local meat and local ale. Serves 4.

Ingredients

For the ox cheeks:

4 ox cheeks

1 dsp English mustard

2 tsp salt

1 tsp white pepper

4 sticks of celery, diced

3 carrots, diced

2 bay leaves

1 sprig of thyme

6 banana shallots, peeled and halved

330ml bottle of Robinson's Old Tom Dark Ale

250ml red wine

1 dsp tomato purée

100g of redcurrant jelly

300ml beef stock (or chicken or vegetable bouillon)

For the celeriac mash:

1 large celeriac

100g unsalted butter

For the turnips:

4 turnips, peeled and cut into wedges

1 tsp olive oil

For the dumplings:

125g self-raising flour

75g suet

2 tbsp horseradish cream

2 sprigs of thyme, picked

1 tsp baking powder

Method

Preheat the oven to 140°C.

For the ox cheeks, rub the cheeks in English mustard and season with one teaspoon of salt and half a teaspoon of white pepper. Add the oil to a heavy frying pan and seal the cheeks, then cook them skin-side down until golden in colour. Set to one side.

In a large baking dish add the diced celery, carrots, bay leaves and thyme. Lay the ox cheeks on top of the vegetables, skin-side up and pack the halved shallots around them.

Pour the ale, red wine, tomato purée and redcurrant jelly into a jug and whisk. This liquor can then be poured over and around the cheeks, but should not cover the skin of the cheeks. Cover the baking dish with a sheet of baking paper and seal it with a layer of kitchen foil.

Put the dish into the preheated oven for 3 hours 45 minutes until the meat is juicy and tender.

For the celeriac mash, peel and dice the celeriac then steam or boil for 30 minutes until soft to pinch. Mash and season with salt and white pepper before adding the butter.

For the turnips, peel the turnips and cut them into wedges. Season with salt and pepper and roast in oil for 25 minutes.

For the dumplings, mix the flour, baking pwder, suet and horseradish cream. Add the picked thyme and drizzle water into the mix until it becomes the consistency of dumplings. Roll into balls the size of a 10 pence piece, making 12-16 dumplings, and set to one side.

Remove the baking dish containing the ox cheeks from the oven. Pour over the beef stock.

Add the dumplings to the baking dish, ensuring they are not touching each other. Put the dish back into the oven, increasing the temperature to 180°C for 10 minutes. For a golden crust, remove the foil lid and cook for a further 10 minutes.

Serve the mash, ox cheek, dumplings and turnips and use the remaining liquor from the baking dish to make a gravy.

A step ABOVE

Renowned for consistently excellent food, Podium restaurant in the Hilton Manchester Deansgate Hotel has been wowing new guests and welcoming back returning customers for nine years.

Podium in Manchester's iconic Hilton Manchester Deansgate Hotel, which towers spectacularly over the city, offers a dining experience with effortless wow factor. The impressive building is intrinsic to Manchester's familiar skyline and the stylish restaurant within has become synonymous with innovative international cuisine and classic British dishes, complemented by some truly local influences.

Executive Head Chef Stuart Duff is a strong supporter of using local producers, believing that it is the best way to ensure you're getting the freshest seasonal ingredients possible and creating the tastiest food. It is for this reason that the menu changes every month, which is also wonderful news for the regular guests who choose to stay and dine at the hotel throughout the year, knowing that there will always be something fresh and original to try. From the full English breakfast featuring Bury black pudding to the Deansgate 'Surf and Turf' fillet of Cheshire beef and grilled lobster, a taste of the north-west runs through the menu.

Executive Head Chef Stuart Duff leads a highly motivated team of young chefs, inspiring them to experiment with both nostalgic flavours and unusual ingredients. The restaurant invests a huge amount of time in its junior chef programme, which is something that everyone at Podium is passionate about. This highly celebrated programme allows for the development of the chefs across the entire kitchen. With support and mentoring from the whole team, and led by the Executive Head Chef, these junior chefs are encouraged to create dishes that are available on the menu each month.

Using suppliers such as Delifresh in Yorkshire, fine cheese specialists Harvey and Brockless and fresh fish supplier Neve's has allowed the chefs to gain incredible knowledge about ingredients, which is reflected in their cooking skills and passion for good-quality food. These suppliers take the chefs to meet farmers and learn about produce, as well as running master classes about specific ingredients.

The glamorous setting is ideal for a cocktail or aperitif before dinner, so the varied mixture of guests can enjoy a leisurely evening to suit their needs or occasion. Open seven days a week, this is a Manchester institution that is set to continue impressing guests to the city and local diners for many years to come.

Podium

TRUFFLE PASTA AND WILD MUSHROOM OPEN LASAGNE WITH WATERCRESS EMULSION

This pasta dish is indulgent and luxurious with its hint of black truffle and creamy wild mushroom filling. You can vary the type of mushrooms used, but always opt for the finest quality you can find. Serves 4.

Ingredients

For the pasta:

200g '00' pasta flour

2 eggs

15g black truffle, grated

For the watercress emulsion:

A bunch of watercress, washed

120ml canola oil

Coarse sea salt and freshly ground black pepper

For the mushrooms:

1 tbsp olive oil

100g good quality wild mushrooms

1 shallot

2 tbsp double cream

Coarse sea salt and freshly ground black pepper

Method

Start by making the pasta. Put the flour on a board and make a well in the middle. Add the eggs and incorporate them into the flour, then add the grated black truffle and knead into a dough. Roll the dough into a ball, wrap in cling film and place in the fridge for 24 hours.

After 24 hours in the fridge, roll out the pasta on a pasta roller machine (or by hand) until thin enough to be transparent. Use a large round cutter to cut the pasta sheets out and place onto a floured tray to stop the pasta sticking.

For the watercress emulsion, remove the thickest stems from the watercress. Bring a medium pot of water to a boil and add 1 tablespoon of salt. Have a medium bowl of ice water at hand for refreshing. When the water returns to the boil, plunge the watercress in and cook for 30 seconds. Drain the watercress and quickly drop into the ice water. When thoroughly chilled, drain the watercress again and lightly squeeze out the water.

Chop the blanched watercress roughly, then place in a blender and purée, adding a little water if necessary to get the mixture going. With the blender running, gradually pour in the canola oil until an emulsion is formed. Add ½ tsp salt and about ¼ tsp pepper, or to taste, then purée again and taste, adjusting the seasoning if needed.

Pick and wash the mushrooms and pat them dry. Heat the oil in a pan and sweat the mushrooms and shallot, then add the cream and reduce to a sauce consistency. Season to taste.

Bring a pan of water to the boil and drop in the truffle pasta discs. Turn down to simmer and cook for 2 minutes, before removing the pasta. Place the pasta discs on a tray and build the lasagne with the mushrooms. Finish with the watercress emulsion and present as per the picture.

Delis with a DIFFERENCE

Two thriving venues with their own distinct personalities – what unites the bustling Pokusevski's Deli in Media City UK and the original site in Heaton Moor is their spotlight on fresh food home-cooked with love and care.

Zoran Pokusevski insists the success of his vibrant eatery in the heart of Media City is down to the incredible team who have brought their love of world cuisines together. Originally from Serbia, Zoran has put world cuisine at the heart of his business, both in the modern hub of Media City and in the more relaxed setting in Heaton Moor.

His close-knit team were carefully selected to bring their individual skills together, giving Pokusevski's a unique dynamic. Each member of the talented team is passionate about food, ingredients and celebrating cuisines from around the world. Head Chef, Moises Catena, brings his Spanish and Jewish culinary heritage to the kitchen, and this is complemented by the other experienced cooks who hail from all over the world, bringing their own amazing influences to the menus. What unites this family of foodies is their love for the best ingredients and tastiest dishes.

Breakfast is an important part of the day, with the Media city fast-movers grabbing a bagel or croissant on their way to the office or indulging in some relaxed celebrity-spotting with eggs florentine or a full English breakfast. The breakfast menu, served till midday, is a real treat.

Heading the baking team at the Heaton Moor site is Paula Maclachlan, who has been tempting the locals with irresistible cakes for over 10 years. Her delights are perfect to be enjoyed with the fine selection of tea and coffee, which makes the relaxing Heaton Moor site a popular place for locals to gather.

The main menu changes regularly, showcasing mouth-watering salads, sandwiches and soups that use the freshest ingredients available that day. From midday, tapas, mezze and pizzas are also on offer, as well as an eclectic mix of main courses such as jerk chicken, spinach and feta filo pie or sticky soy salmon with honey and chilli. The ever-changing specials often include Middle Eastern platters of home-made flatbreads, falafel, tabbouleh, hummus and baba ganoush – and since Pokusevski's is open into the evenings, too, you can sit back with a glass of wine and sample the menu at your leisure.

Pokusevskis
CHEFS BREAKFAST

This breakfast was created by our Head Chef Moises. It's a gentle fusion of Mediterranean and Oriental cuisine and it has become one of the most popular breakfasts in our Media City store. It is also very pleasing on the eye, particularly on a coloured plate. Serves 2.

Ingredients

6 small garlic cloves

A small bunch of parsley (4 tablespoons when chopped), plus extra for decorating

6 tbsp extra virgin olive oil

2 slices good-quality white bread

4 slices Serrano ham

4 large, free-range, organic eggs

For the topping:

2 ripe but firm vine tomatoes

½ small red onion

30ml extra virgin olive oil, plus a little extra for frying

15ml Balsamic vinegar

1 tsp honey

For the sauce:

50ml oyster sauce

1 tsp dark soy sauce

1 tbsp cider vinegar

Method

Preheat the oven to 180°C (fan 160°F).

Start by preparing the topping. Chop the tomatoes and onion into small cubes. In a large bowl, mix the extra virgin olive oil, balsamic vinegar and honey. Add the tomatoes and onions and mix well. Leave to rest. (Any leftover mixture will keep in the fridge for up to 3 days and can be used as a topping for bruschetta.)

Next, make the sauce by mixing all the ingredients together. (The sauce will keep for up to 30 days in the fridge.)

Crush two of the garlic cloves and mix with 3 tablespoons of the chopped parsley. Grind them together using a pestle and mortar or blitz in a food processor. Add 2 tablespoons of the extra virgin olive oil and mix well. Spread the mixture on top of the bread, place on a baking tray and bake in the preheated oven for approximately 3 minutes until nice and crisp.

At the same time, spread the Serrano ham on a separate baking tray and bake for approximately 3 minutes until firm and crispy, if you like it that way.

Heat a non-stick frying pan with the remaining 4 tablespoons extra virgin olive oil and fry the eggs, leaving the yolk still runny. Remove the eggs and place on a warmed plate.

Finely chop the remaining four garlic cloves and add them to the frying pan. Fry gently until golden and crispy, but not burnt. Remove with a slotted spoon.

Arrange the crispy bread and Serrano ham on two plates. Top the bread with the tomato and onion mixture. Sprinkle crispy garlic and the remaining finely chopped fresh parsley on the top of fried eggs. To finish, drizzle generously with the sauce.

Pokusevskis
COURGETTE AND LEMON CAKE

This is a wonderfully light and moist cake. It is one of the most popular cakes with our customers in both of our places, Heaton Moor and Media City UK. You will need a 23cm lined cake tin. Serves 12.

Ingredients

340g butter, softened

340g caster sugar

Zest of 1 lemon, finely grated, plus extra to decorate

1 tsp vanilla extract

6 large, free-range, organic eggs

340g self-raising flour

1 medium courgette, about 300g, finely grated

2 tsp baking powder

For the icing:

150g soft cream cheese

100g icing sugar

2 tbsp lemon curd

Long thin strips of lemon zest to decorate

Method

Preheat the oven to 180°C (fan 160°F).

Beat together the butter, sugar, lemon zest and vanilla until pale and fluffy. Add two of the eggs and beat together, then add a little of the flour and beat again. Add the remaining four eggs and beat well. Fold in the remaining flour carefully. Fold in the grated courgette and the baking powder.

Spoon the mixture into a lined 23cm cake tin and bake in the preheated oven for 50 minutes or until a skewer inserted into the centre of the cake comes out clean. Leave to cool.

Meanwhile, mix together the icing ingredients. Spoon the icing onto the cooled cake and decorate with extra freshly grated lemon zest.

Burton ROSE

Since opening in 2011, The Rose Garden, named in memory of the owner's mum Rose, has already earned its place in the Good Food Guide and Michelin Guide – setting itself apart as one of Burton Road's most renowned restaurants.

Nestled in the heart of West Didsbury, the cosmopolitan Burton road is the perfect spot for this family-run restaurant. Run by dedicated husband and wife team William Mills and Emma Caress, this award-winning eatery has risen from new start-up to highly acclaimed restaurant in just a few short years. None of this would have been possible without the unwavering support of mum and dad Clare and George and siblings Tom, Joe and Chloë, who all contributed to its successful start.

In their first six months of opening The Rose Garden was nominated for Best Newcomer in the Manchester Food and Drink Awards, and then for Best Restaurant the following year, demonstrating just how quickly this little family-run restaurant went from local gem to Manchester-wide favourite. Today, after an exciting period of expansion into the upstairs area, they are proud to not only be listed in the Good Food Guide and Michelin Guide, but to have been awarded their first AA rosette.

So what is it about this popular spot that keeps the accolades coming? The bright atmosphere is welcoming and modern – clean and fresh and light, the white tables are decorated with a simple rose, adding a splash of colour to the contemporary setting. Emma managed the front of house for the first couple of years and today splits her time between caring for their two-year-old son and day-time front of house, maintaining the effortlessly modern and fresh atmosphere for which the restaurant is known.

Head Chef William endeavours to use seasonal produce and chooses the best suppliers Manchester has to offer. He changes his menu frequently to reflect the local seasonal produce he has at his fingertips, and this gives the loyal regulars something new and exciting to try each time they visit. The wine list has been thoughtfully compiled using two of their favourite suppliers – a neighbouring wine shop, Reserve Wines, and a Yorkshire wine merchant, Buon Vino, who source organic and biodynamic wines.

For William, it's all about keeping things interesting and fresh for customers, and one way is by putting on taster nights: "We will team up with one of our wine suppliers and produce a matched food and wine evening. We have recently done an English wines taster, a foraging taster and a summer holidays taster." Keep an eye on the website for more exciting events in the future.

The Rose Garden

PARMA HAM-WRAPPED MONKFISH TAIL, PEA MOUSSE, BATTERED MONKFISH CHEEK, CLAM SALSA

This is a show-stopping celebration of sweet peas and fresh monkfish. Created by William Mills. Head Chef at The Rose Garden. Serves 4.

Ingredients

800g monkfish tail

8 slices Parma ham

100g butter, plus extra for basting

Juice of ½ lemon

Buttered peas, to serve

Pea shoots, to serve

Salt and Pepper

For the pea mousse:

50ml milk

200ml double cream

150g blanched peas

3g agar agar

For the battered monkfish cheek:

50g cornflour

100g plain flour, plus extra for dusting

3g instant yeast

¼ tsp turmeric

1 tsp salt

200ml sparkling water

4 monkfish cheeks

For the clam salsa:

75ml olive oil

25ml white wine vinegar

Juice of ½ lemon

1 clove garlic, crushed

100g clams, cooked and removed from shell

1 tsp chopped parsley

1 tsp capers

2 plum tomatoes, peeled, deseeded and chopped

1 shallot, peeled and finely chopped

For the pea tuile:

75g sugar

110g butter, melted and cooled

70g plain flour

3 egg whites

50g blanched peas, puréed and passed through a sieve

Method

Cut the monkfish tail into four equal portions. Take two pieces of Parma ham and roll them out between two pieces of cling film. Melt the butter and add the lemon juice and salt and pepper. Using a pastry brush, spread butter over the Parma ham, then place a piece of monkfish tail at the bottom end of the ham and roll it tightly. Tie the ends of the cling film. Repeat with the rest of the tails and then refrigerate for at least an hour.

For the pea mousse, warm the milk and cream to near boiling point, then remove from the heat and add the blanched peas and agar agar. Blend with a hand blender until smooth and pass through a sieve. Pour into cling film-lined rings and leave to set in the fridge for at least 2 hours.

For the battered monkfish cheeks, put the flours, yeast and turmeric into a bowl, add the salt, then whisk in the sparkling water. Cover with cling film and leave the batter in a warm place for 30-45 minutes. Season the cheeks with salt and pepper and then dust in plain flour. Drop the cheeks into the batter, ready for frying later.

For the clam salsa, gradually add the olive oil to the white wine vinegar whilst whisking. Add the lemon juice, garlic, clams, parsley, capers, tomatoes and shallots. Season to taste and leave to infuse for at least 30 minutes.

For the pea tuile, mix together all the ingredients and leave to cool in the fridge for at least an hour. Preheat the oven to 180°C. Spread the tuile mix into a rectangular template on a heatproof silicon sheet, and put in the preheated oven for 6-9 minutes until starting to colour very slightly at edges. Remove from the sheet and, whilst still hot, wrap around a metal ring and leave to cool.

To assemble, heat a deep-fryer to 180°C. Remove the monkfish from the cling film. Heat a pan and sear the monkfish tail on all sides then place in the oven for 6-10 minutes depending on the thickness of the tail. Remove the pea mousse from the ring and distribute the salsa over it, then place it inside the tuile and on a plate. Drop the cheeks carefully into the deep-fryer and cook until golden brown; about 5-6 minutes. Remove the monkfish from the oven and baste with butter. Slice into equal medallions and place on plate. Add a battered cheek, a few buttered peas and some pea shoots, and then drizzle with the dressing from the clam salsa.

The Rose Garden
RHUBARB AND GINGER

This recipe by Hannah Widdowson, pastry chef at the rose garden, comprises poached Yorkshire forced rhubarb batons, ginger beer jelly, dehydrated meringue drops, vanilla panna cotta, lemon curd, ginger biscuit crumble and rhubarb sorbet. Serves 8.

Ingredients

For the rhubarb sorbet: (Makes 2 Litres)

500g rhubarb puree

260g sugar

For the meringue drops:

500g sugar

6 egg whites

For the ginger beer jelly:

225g caster sugar

500ml ginger beer

8 gelatine leaves, soaked in cold water

For the vanilla pannacotta:

Seeds of 2 vanilla pods

425ml double cream

125ml milk

85g caster sugar

3 gelatine leaves, soaked in cold water

For the lemon curd: (Makes 1 jam jar)

100g butter, cubed

Zest and juice of 4 lemons

200g sugar

3 eggs and 1 egg yolk

For the ginger biscuit crumble:

340g plain flour

1 tsp bicarbonate of soda

2 tsp ground ginger

100g butter

160g light brown sugar

4 tbsp golden syrup

1 egg, beaten

For the poached rhubarb:

100g sugar

1 lemon, halved

10g fresh ginger, grated

1 drop pink food colouring

1 stick of rhubarb, cut into 3cm batons

Method

For the rhubarb sorbet, heat the sugar and 370ml water in a pan. Boil for a couple of minutes. Add the purée. Place in the freezer to set and leave overnight. The next day place the sorbet into a food processor and mix. Store back in the freezer.

For the meringue drops, add the sugar and 250ml water to a pan, bring to the boil and take to 121°C on a sugar thermometer. Place the egg whites into a stand mixer. When the syrup reaches 111°C, start to whisk the whites. Pour the stock syrup over the egg whites and mix on medium-high setting until cool. This will form a glossy Italian meringue. Place some of the meringue into a piping bag with nozzle. Pipe onto a tray lined with baking parchment, leaving gaps between each meringue. Place in a dehydrator for 12 hours until crisp. Or place right at the bottom of an oven set at 70°C for 4 hours.

For the ginger beer jelly, place the sugar, beer and 725ml water into a pan. Bring to the boil. Take off the heat and let the gelatine dissolve. Pass through a sieve and set in moulds or a tray lined with cling film.

For the vanilla pannacotta, place all the ingredients except the gelatine into a pan and bring to the boil. Place the gelatine leaves in the hot mixture to dissolve. Pass the mixture through a sieve and set in moulds. Place in the refrigerator and set for at least 4 hours.

For the lemon curd, place the butter in a heatproof bowl with the lemon zest, juice and sugar. Set over a bain marie and stir with a whisk until the butter has melted. Beat the eggs and add them to the lemon mixture. Cook for 10 minutes, whisking occasionally. The curd should feel heavy on the whisk and be custard-like. Take off the heat and allow to cool before storing.

For the ginger biscuit crumble, preheat the oven to 180°C and line a tray with baking parchment.

Place all the dry ingredients into a bowl and rub the butter in. This will look like breadcrumbs. Stir in the sugar, then the syrup and egg. Bring to form a smooth dough. Roll out the dough onto a lightly floured surface, about 2cm thick, cut out the biscuits using a cutter. Bake for 15 minutes. Once the biscuits have cooled, crush them by hand or whiz them in a food processor. Place the crumble back onto a tray and cook for a further 5 minutes.

For the poached rhubarb, place everything except the rhubarb into a pan with 200ml water and bring to the boil. Bring the poaching liquid to a simmer and place the rhubarb in the pan. Leave to poach for half an hour on a very low heat; be careful not to boil it.

Plate up all the elements as shown in the picture.

Little ITALY

For a laid-back, family-run taste of southern Italy in Manchester, look no further than Salvi's Cucina, Salvi's Rosticceria and the revamped Salvi's Mozzarella Bar in the new Corn Exchange.

Husband and wife team Claire and Maurizio – the owners of Salvi's – are passionate about all things southern Italian. Although they couldn't quite bring the sunshine to Manchester, they have certainly thought of everything else that makes the food of Maurizio's home country so completely enchanting.

Salvi's is a family affair like no other. Maurizio's love of food began in his mother's kitchen in Naples, the home of some of the world's finest ingredients. Having been a chef in the north-west for many years, Maurizio decided it was time to share the secrets of his birth place with his new home town of Manchester. His brother Emiliano's famous mozzarella was a must, of course, and, armed with some of the best produce Naples has to offer and the promise of his mother's secret recipes, he opened Salvi's in Manchester's Corn Exchange… and named it after his father, Salvatore.

Today Maurizio and his wife Claire have three authentic venues that celebrate the very finest Italian produce. Salvi's Cucina offers rustic Neapolitan food that is simple yet elegant,

overseen by a team of Italian chefs (who are occasionally joined by Maurizio's mum Teresa!) in the theatrical open kitchen. Salvi's Rosticceria is the place to grab food on the run – the Italians insist on every eating experience being a great one and so do the team here. Freshly made pizza slices, arancini, lasagne, polpette, risotto, calzone or frittata can all be taken away, along with an irresistible doughnut, cake or coffee of course.

The jewel in the crown is the new space in the Corn Exchange, which now has its own restaurant downstairs, as well as the Italian deli upstairs, and one of Manchester's finest outdoor drinking and dining spaces, too, on Exchange Square.

Downstairs, as well as intimate, relaxed dining, guests can also enjoy tastings and master classes, or simply indulge in a plate or two of fine Italian cheese. Sharing boards, fantastic wines, authentic lunches and gorgeous dinners all abound at this new 'Super Salvi's', making this newly developed space one of the most exciting places to enjoy authentic Italian food in Manchester.

Salvi's
POLPO ALLA LUCIANA

Fresh octopus cooked in a Mediterranean tomato sauce with
capers and black olives. Serves 4.

Ingredients

1200g fresh cleaned octopus

4 tbsp olive oil

4 cloves garlic

1 small fresh red chilli, sliced

2 spoonfuls of black pitted olives

1 tbsp capers

500g tinned cherry tomatoes

1 small glass of white wine

1 bunch of parsley, chopped

Salt and pepper

Method

Make sure the octopus is clean and washed. Place the octopus in a pan of boiling water and allow to cook for 20 minutes. Remove octopus from the pan and drain. Allow to cool and chop into small sections, approximately 2cm cubed.

Place the olive oil, garlic, sliced chilli, olives and capers in a large pan. Add the tinned cherry tomatoes and stir together.

Add the octopus and white wine and allow to cook. Add salt and pepper to season. Once boiling, reduce to a simmer and cook for 30 minutes. Add the parsley once simmering.

Serve with warm crusty bread, drizzled in olive oil.

Simon Wood's
BALLOTINE OF CHICKEN

wrapped in Parma ham with linguine and arrabiata sauce.

Since being crowned the winner of MasterChef UK 2015, Simon Wood has had a whirlwind year. He is currently the Executive Chef at Oldham Athletic, where he has developed the 'Simon Wood Menu'. "Smoky, spicy arrabiata sauce is a simple classic and always popular. Although the ballotine serves two people, I tend to make a big portion of sauce and freeze the leftovers – my freezer is full of pasta sauces! I use linguine here, but you can use any other pasta shape you have to hand." Serves 2.

Ingredients

1 chicken breast

3 slices of Parma ham

Olive oil

A knob of butter

Linguine, to serve

Pea shoots, to decorate

For the arrabiata sauce:

80g pancetta lardons

5 shallots, diced

2 cloves smoked garlic, crushed

1 tsp chilli oil

5 vine tomatoes

35g fresh basil

1½ tsp smoked paprika

1 litre passata

1 tin chopped tomatoes

Sea salt and coarse ground black pepper

For the filling:

½ chicken breast

½ chorizo sausage

A small bunch of basil

1 tbsp mascarpone

Method

To make the arrabiata sauce, add the pancetta lardons to a frying pan with a little oil and brown gently. Next add the diced shallots, and then add the crushed smoked garlic and continue to cook. Add a pinch of pepper and a drizzle of chilli oil. Chop the vine tomatoes and basil, and add to frying pan, then add the smoked paprika, passata and chopped tomatoes, bring to a simmer and cook for 10-15 minutes. Season to taste. Blitz the sauce in a food processor until smooth, then pass the sauce through a sieve, and return to the frying pan. Check the seasoning and adjust accordingly. Cover and set aside, ready to reheat for serving.

To make the filling, blitz the filling ingredients together in a food processor to a smooth paté. (You can use this mixture for meatballs for a super quick dinner – my kids love them. Simply increase the quantities to make more of the mixture.)

Take the chicken breast and place it on a chopping board. With one hand flat on top of the breast, use a sharp knife to cut through the breast, being careful not to cut all the way through to the other side. Open out the chicken breast into a butterfly shape. Cover it with a sheet of cling film and use a rolling pin to bash it gently to an even thickness.

Place a sheet of cling film on a clean board and place the Parma ham slices on top with no gaps. Place the butterflied breast on top. Take the filling and spoon it in a line down the centre of the chicken. Using the cling film, roll the chicken breast up into a sausage shape, then twist the cling film at both ends to secure it (like wrapping up a sweet).

Bring a pan of water to the boil and place the cling film-wrapped chicken in. Simmer for 20 minutes, resting a ladle on the chicken ballotine to hold it under the water if it starts to float.

Remove the ballotine from the water using a slotted spoon and allow to cool for a few moments. Carefully remove the cling film.

Meanwhile, cook the linguine according to the packet instructions and heat up the arrabiata sauce. The arrabiata sauce will make enough for 4 servings, so you can freeze half at this stage.

Heat a frying pan over medium heat and add a little oil. Add the ballotine of chicken to the pan and cook, turning, until browned on all sides. Add a knob of butter to the pan for the last 2 minutes. Slice the ballotine into 1.5cm slices. Serve the linguine with the arrabiata sauce and top each portion with a few slices of chicken ballotine. Decorate with a few pea shoots.

A Slice of ROME

Slice Pizza & Bread Bar has brought the secrets of pizza by the slice, or "pizza al taglio" from the streets of Rome to Manchester's buzzing Northern Quarter.

Matt McGuirk, the man behind this little Italian gem in Stevenson Square, is truly passionate about pizza. Matt originally wanted to start a business based on creating good, honest food from scratch and to break free from the large chains that monopolise many of our city centres today. As he was a huge fan of real Italian pizza, he set about developing what the perfect pizza meant to him, and he soon became fascinated by the history of pizza al taglio (which literally means pizza by the cut and is traditionally sold by weight).

When the British pizza fan arrived in Rome to train – to the amazement of many locals! – it was difficult to find anyone to share the secrets of this ancient craft with him. Eventually Matt was introduced to a pizzeria by the owner of the guest house in which he was staying. After promising that he would not be sharing any secrets with any Roman competition, he was allowed into the kitchen to learn the art of pizza making with master pizzaiolo Emiliano Baldini.

In his spare time, he ate his way around the city, sampling pizza from every pizzeria possible and learning as much as he could about the dough. On arrival back in Manchester, bespoke pizza ovens were ordered from the famous Castelli Forni in Lazio and Slice Pizza & Bread Bar began to take shape.

The premises have that unmistakable feel of Rome when you enter. The counter displays the sumptuous pizzas all made fresh each day with carefully considered toppings such as Mozzarella, Potato and Rosemary; Scamorza Affumicata, Mushroom and Sausage; or the favourite choice Mozzarella, Broccoli, Sausage and Chilli. Baked in large rectangular trays, your slice will be heated to order in one of the hand-made Castelli Forni ovens, which ensures you will always enjoy a crisp base beneath the generous toppings.

Having won Best Pizzeria at the English Italian Awards and coming second to Gino D'Acampo at the Pizza Pasta Awards, this little micro-business has quickly become one of Manchester's most exciting dining destinations. With focaccia, panini and nutella-filled calzone also on offer, plus fresh gelato and a selection of drinks at the bar, they are slowly expanding from a busy pizza counter into a larger dining space where you can enjoy a slice of pizza with a cold beer or a relaxed aperitivo Italian-style.

Slice Pizzeria

MOZZARELLA, BROCCOLI, SAUSAGE AND CHILLI PIZZA

This pizza has been a best-seller at Slice since we opened. It's the pizza people always write about and recommend others to try for the first time. At Slice we use huge purpose-built ovens and can bake the pizza at specific temperatures. With a little work you can get great results at home. The dough technique seems complicated but it just takes practice. I have based this recipe on a standard 13 x 18 inch baking tray with sides. The thinner the better as it will make the base crispier. The sides help to hold the sides of the stretched base in place. Makes 3.

Ingredients

500g good-quality bread flour ('tipo 0' if you can get it)

3g brewers instant yeast

350ml water, room temperature (if you live in an area with very hard water use bottled water)

20ml extra virgin olive oil (a deep-coloured, good-quality one), plus extra for oiling

10g salt (fine sea salt is best)

Finely milled semolina (optional)

1 tsp sunflower oil, for oiling

For the topping (per pizza):

400g mozzarella (rather than buy the grated stuff, buy a block and cut it into 1cm cubes)

500g cooked broccoli (the fresher the better, boiled with the lid off in salted water to keep a deep green colour)

400g good-quality sausages with high pork content

Extra virgin olive oil

5 red chillis, finely diced

Salt and pepper

Method

Mix the flour and yeast in a wooden bowl using a wooden spoon. This aerates the flour and starts to get the yeast working. Pour in the water, a little at the time, mixing until a rough batter is created. You can at this stage start to see the gluten strands forming the structure of the dough. Add the extra virgin olive oil and salt and mix to incorporate. The oil may look like it is curdling the mixture, but keep going and it will mix in. If the salt is added earlier, it can inhibit the enzymes in the yeast. You will now have a rough, lumpy dough. Place in an oiled mixing bowl, cover with a tea towel and leave at room temperature for 1 hour.

Turn the dough out onto a floured surface (a wooden work top or a large wooden chopping board is ideal). Now to incorporate as much air as possible into the dough. Pull the bottom edge of the dough up and fold it into the middle like wrapping a present, then do the same with the top, folding that towards you. Turn the dough 90° and then fold the bottom, then top, in on each other again. Repeat three times. The texture of the dough should look smoother. Turn the dough over so the folded seam is on the bottom and gently form it into a rough ball with your palms.

Repeat this process every 15 minutes for 1 hour, leaving the dough on the floured surface during this process.

Place the dough, seam-side down, in a large oiled bowl and coat the top of the dough with some olive oil to stop a skin from forming. Cover with a tea towel and leave on the bottom shelf of the fridge for 24 hours.

After 24 hours, turn the bowl upside down onto a floured work top. Leave it for 15 minutes to come up to room temperature. Using a bench scraper or knife, weigh and portion the dough out. Customers at Slice like a really thin crispy pizza, so I'd portion it out in 300g pieces.

Try to handle the dough as little as possible as you don't want to knock out all of the air pockets and bubbles you have created. Then repeat the folding you did the day before, but just once. Round the dough into a ball again and leave on the floured work surface to rest for 1½ hours.

Preheat the oven to 250°C. Oil the baking tray (sunflower oil is fine). Gently place the dough on a floured the work surface (at Slice we use semolina to give the base a rough texture). Gently manipulate the dough with your fingertips into a rectangle, remembering to keep the bubbles intact. When training I was told to imagine the high arched fingers of a concert pianist when doing this.

Sometimes, when I'm training them, my staff struggle getting the stretched base into the tray for the first time, but it just takes practice. Get one of the short ends of the rectangle facing towards you, cross your left arm diagonally over the pizza to the far right corner of the dough then use your right hand to fold the dough over your left arm. Now, support the underneath of the right side with back of your other arm, so both arms are straight out in front of you. By shaking your arms you'll stretch the dough a little and shake off any excess flour or semolina. Gently ease it into the corners of the tray.

Put a layer of mozzarella on the pizza right up to the edges, leaving a 1cm gap between the cubes. Mash and tear the broccoli with your fingertips and then cover the top of the mozzarella with broccoli. Rip the sausage skins off and mould the meat into balls in the palms of your hands (I usually get three balls from one sausage). Sprinkle over salt and pepper and extra virgin olive oil.

Bake in the preheated oven for about 25 minutes until the crust is well risen and the topping is cooked. You can use a palette knife to lift up the pizza from the side and see how the base is looking. It should be golden brown on the bottom with the beginnings of dots of char. Sprinkle with chillies and serve.

The Perfect Bowl Of NOODLES

Manchester's original, independent Pan Asian restaurant celebrates an exciting new chapter as the stunning Corn Exchange venue re-launches in style.

Mouth-watering tastes, aromas and textures from across Asia were first served up in Manchester back in 1997, when Tampopo opened on Albert Square. It was an instant love affair, as the food-loving city took this fresh, vibrant restaurant to its heart.

Named after the eponymous heroine in a Japanese film, who was searching for the perfect bowl of noodles, the Tampopo philosophy remains unchanged from when it launched - the founders are still on their own quest to provide Manchester with the very best traditional Asian food.

Co-Founder David Fox has travelled throughout East Asia, attending cooking schools in Indonesia, Thailand, Malaysia and Vietnam. Seduced by the culinary traditions and fresh ingredients of these countries, he decided to bring the authentic tastes back to the city he calls home.

Fresh and delicious food is the key to Tampopo's success, with customers always treated to a simple and fuss-free dining experience. High-quality ingredients are at the core of the business, with stocks and sauces made fresh, daily on site. Despite the commitment to using the freshest ingredients, the restaurant's prices remain more than competitive.

Whether it's a bowl of pad Thai - carefully balanced between hot, sour, salty and sweet - or a portion of Japanese dumplings known as gyoza, all the dishes are true to their roots and are packed with the authentic herbs and spices you'd expect if you were eating them at a night market in Asia.

It's this passion and commitment that means Tampopo stands out from its rivals. Despite having expanded to two more Manchester sites - at the Trafford Centre and the Corn Exchange - it is still a firm favourite in the city 19 years after opening. Over the decades various celebrities have sat at its long communal benches to enjoy the tasty food on offer. Tony Wilson very quickly became a friend and loyal supporter (his favourite dish was coconut prawn). Local heroes ranging from Ian Brown to Christopher Eccleston have been known to pop in for a quick bite, while Inspiral Carpets front man Clint Boon held his wedding lunch at Tampopo Albert Square. Touring actors/performers such as Billy Connolly, Uri Geller and Jason Donovan have sampled Tampopo dishes, along with the likes of David Beckham and Rio Ferdinand.

The latest chapter in the Tampopo success story is the re-launch of its Corn Exchange branch. The building's redevelopment has breathed new life into this historic part of the city and Tampopo sits proudly at its heart. A bright and vibrant space that is bursting with life, it is the perfect place to enjoy some exotic cuisine; from a quick meal to an intimate lunch in one of the cosy alcoves, the new Corn Exchange restaurant means that Tampopo just got a little bit more glamorous!

Tampopo

Tampopo's
THAI MUSSELS TOM YAM STYLE

No flavours take me to Thailand more than tom yam. Hot, salty, sour and sweet in each mouthful. Serves 4 as a starter.

Ingredients

32 mussels, cleaned

8 cherry tomatoes, cut into quarters

16 Asian basil leaves

16 coriander sprigs roughly chopped

8 slices large chilli

For the tom yam stock:

560ml good vegetable stock

4 tbsp fish sauce

2 tbsp light soy sauce

1 small bird's eye chilli, finely chopped

3 lime leaves

2 pieces lemongrass stalks finely chopped

2 tbsp finely chopped coriander

½ teaspoon ginger

Juice of a whole lime

1 tsp sugar

2 pinches of salt

Method

To make the tom yam stock

Add all the ingredients to a wok with the vegetable stock and bring to the boil.

For the mussels

Add the mussels and tomatoes to the stock and cover for a few minutes or until the mussels have opened.

Add the Asian basil leaves, coriander sprigs and slices of chilli to infuse the stock.

Serve in cute little bowls and enjoy the slurps around the table.

Tampopo's
VEGETABLE TEMPURA

This dish sums up so much of Japanese cuisine.
Simple and delicious! Serves 4 as a starter.

Ingredients

2 carrot batons

2 red peppers cut into triangles

2 pieces of baby corn, cut lengthways

2 long green beans

2 slices of sweet potato

2 inches white radish

Sunflower oil, for frying

For the tempura batter mix:

150g tempura flour (from any good Chinese supermarket, if you cannot get hold of tempura flour use 60g cornflour, 90g plain flour and 6g baking powder)

200ml cold water (some recipes use sparkling water, we don't!)

For the tempura sauce:

200ml dashi stock (made from scratch or use dashi powder from a Chinese supermarket)

2 tbsp mirin

2 tsp sugar

2 tbsp soy sauce

Method

For the tempura sauce, combine the dashi stock, mirin, sugar and soy sauce in a small saucepan and bring to a boil. Then lower the heat and let it simmer until the sugar is completely dissolved. Remove from heat and set aside.

For the tempura batter mix, sift the tempura flour into a bowl so that it is lump-free. Add the water and mix with a spoon to ensure that it is lump-free. Do not whisk it. When done, the batter mix should coat your finger. Chill in the fridge, ensuring it is completely chilled before use.

To cook the tempura, heat enough sunflower oil to just cover the vegetables to 190°C in a wok or similar. (Do not over fill with oil, as it can be dangerous.)

Coat the vegetables in the tempura batter mix. Pick up each piece of vegetable with chopsticks and lower onto the surface of the oil and lightly move from side-to-side for a couple of seconds before releasing into the oil. Cook for 3 minutes until cooked through but with still with a slight bite. Remove from fryer and shake off any excess oil. Transfer the vegetables to a bowl with paper towels to drain off any excess oil.

Place the vegetables on a serving plate with dipping tray and serve.

Tampopo's
THAI BASIL IN A FIERY OYSTER SAUCE

Pad Krapow

The spiciness is offset by the sweetness of the oyster sauce and the savoury of the fish sauce, with the Asian basil coming through shouting, "I'm here too!". You can use chicken (We prefer thighs) or aubergine instead of prawns, if you like. Serves 4 as a main.

Ingredients

2 tbsp vegetable oil

400g sliced onion

200g chopped green beans

3 small birds eye chillies, finely chopped (you can use large chillies, or a mix, to soften the spice)

3 tbsp garlic, finely chopped

48 blanched prawns (butterflied, if you can – they look nicer and they cook better)

4 tbsp oyster sauce

4 teaspoons sugar

4 tbsp dark soy sauce

3 tbsp fish sauce

3 tbsp lime juice

3 tbsp water

400ml sliced red pepper

40 Thai basil leaves

To garnish:

6 fried Thai basil leaves

2 pieces of sliced chilli

Method

Heat the oil in a wok. Add the onion and green beans and stir-fry for 30 seconds. Add the chilli and garlic and stir-fry on low heat for 10 seconds. Add the blanched butterflied prawns and stir-fry for 30 seconds.

Add the oyster sauce, sugar, soy sauce, fish sauce, lime juice and water and bring to the boil, stirring constantly. Reduce the heat and simmer for 30 seconds or until sauce has reduced by one-third.

Add the red pepper and Thai basil leaves and stir for 10 seconds.

Turn onto a plate, garnish with fried Thai basil leaves, sliced chilli and serve.

Time FOR TEA

As any Brit knows, the perfect cup of tea needs the perfect teatime treat to serve alongside it, but at Teacup Kitchen, the innovative menu is starting to steal the show.

Thomas Street in the hub of Manchester's trendy Northern Quarter is home to the unique eatery that celebrates Britain's favourite drink, along with the incredible food that accompanies it. Owned by acclaimed Manchester DJ Mr. Scruff and Gary McClarnan, Teacup Kitchen began life as a record shop nearly a decade ago. It has since been transformed into a foodie hotspot by the two self-declared tea enthusiasts, who have put speciality loose-leaf teas and top-quality food at the heart and soul of this quirky venue.

There is no doubt they offer a unique experience for the tea fanatic. Not only do they have one of the widest ranges of loose-leaf tea in Manchester, they serve them with a special timer for each pot to ensure that you get the perfect brew every time – while adding a fun twist to your cuppa.

The impressive menu is down to inspirational kitchen staff, having won "Best Brunches in Manchester" on Creative Tourist and "The Most Innovative Breakfast in 2015" in The Breakfast Week Awards on the blog Shake Up Your Wake Up, for their original Exoticado. Luckily, breakfast is served all day, so whether it's mid-morning or mid-afternoon, you can enjoy their belting benedict or dippy duck eggs. wraps,

sandwiches, pies and soup are also on the menu for lunch, incorporating flavours from around the world but sourcing ingredients from as close to home as possible.

Of course it's the eye-catching cakes that draw in many a customer – the rainbow cake with its layers of multi-coloured sponge is a firm favourite, but choosing between classic scones, gooey brownies and flourless chocolate cake proves tricky for many! The afternoon tea allows you to sit down and enjoy finger sandwiches, savoury treats, mini cakes, tarts and scones – three tiers of deliciousness served with a pot of tea or a glass of bubbles.

Teacup Kitchen, along with Bonbon Chocolate Boutique, Proper Tea at Manchester Cathedral and The Cafe at The Museum, is part of the Casual Manna family, which is putting proper tea and good food at the heart of Manchester's culinary scene. Having featured in The Good Food Guide for three years in a row and won "Best Casual Dining Venue of the Year 2012" at the prestigious Manchester Food & Drink Awards, Teacup is also listed as one of "Britain's 25 Best Places to Eat at the Weekend" by The Times. It's clear that Manchester's thirst for all things tea has not been quenched yet.

Teacup Kitchen's
EXOTICADO

Listed as one of the "Best Brunches in Manchester" on Creative Tourist and winner of "The Most Innovative Breakfast in 2015" in The Breakfast Week Awards on the blog Shake Up Your Wake Up, this breakfast dish comprises a luxurious duck egg, avocado and wild mushrooms on sourdough. Serves 1.

Ingredients

30g butter

200g wild mushrooms

150g avocado, peeled and stoned

Lemon juice

1 duck egg

Sourdough toast

Sea salt

Method

Heat a frying pan, add the butter and cook until a golden brown, then add the mushrooms and fry them in the butter for about 2 minutes. Finally add the fresh avocado, lemon juice and season with salt.

To poach the duck egg, bring a pan of water to the boil and add the lemon juice. Once the water is boiling, create a whirlpool in the water then crack the duck egg into the water. Cook for around 2 minutes.

Serve the mushroom and avocado on sourdough toast with the poached duck egg.

Teacup Kitchen's
FLOURLESS CHOCOLATE CAKE

One of the favourite cakes at Teacup, this recipe is ideal for
those who avoid eating gluten. Makes 1 cakes.

Ingredients

400g 53% chocolate

142g 70% chocolate

360g butter

490g eggs, separated (about 10 eggs)

435g Muscovado sugar

90g water

Seeds of 1 vanilla pod

A pinch of salt

Method

Line a 10" springform mould with non-stick baking parchment and set aside. Preheat oven to 120°C

Melt the chocolate and the butter in a water bath over a medium-low heat, stirring constantly to prevent scorching of the chocolate.

Set aside to cool slightly, but make sure it doesn't cool down completely and set.

Carefully separate the eggs into whites & yolks.

Combine the whites, sugar, water & vanilla and whisk on the highest speed in a stand mixer until glossy and forming stiff peaks.

Whisk the yolks into the warm melted chocolate mixture.

Carefully fold the whites into the chocolate and yolks, aiming to keep as much volume as possible.

Transfer the mix into a 10inch spring form mould.

Cover with a heavy baking tray or tin foil and bake at 120 °C for 2 hours, then leave to cool in the oven.

Refrigerate for at least 6 hours, or overnight if possible.

Treasure TROVE

Artisan sourdough loaves sold from the bakery and beautiful, hand-made food from their gorgeous Levenshulme café, Trove is true to its name, housing an utterly lovely collection of delightful goodies.

The Trove story began in 2011 when Katy and Marcus Saide began selling their home-made chutneys and jams on market stalls around Manchester. What began as a simple love of quality, additive-free, local produce has never changed, but the husband and wife team have now grown into a group of passionate foodies – all of whom have united over these simple core values.

They were given the opportunity to take over a tiny café space in Levenshulme, where they started to make their own sourdough loaves. Organic ingredients were a must and their incredible hand-made sourdough bread proved extremely popular on the café menu.

As the demand for their artisan sourdough loaves increased, they found their café kitchen simply couldn't cope with the wholesale orders they were now fulfilling for a plethora of local businesses. The Trove team now have a separate bakery just 5 minutes away from their thriving café where they can focus on baking their popular products, which range from sourdough and rye to croissants and fruit tarts. The ethos of the bakery is run with the same core ethic as the café – everything is made from scratch using the finest organic ingredients and, of course, with no nasty additives.

The café kitchen is still where everything that is sold in the café is made, from the hollandaise for their famous eggs benedict to the salting of the beef for the bagels. True to their roots, the home-made chutneys and jams are still created here and are as popular as ever with the regulars – in fact they jar up any preserves they make and you'll spot them on the shelves, so you can always buy a jar to take home after lunch. The irresistible home-made cake selection is made fresh on site each day too, and the talented bakers can make cakes to order.

PAIN au RAISIN
···· £1.50 ····

KANELBULLAR
CARDAMOM + CINNAMON
KNOTS
£2

FINANCIER
£1.50

FLORENTINE
£1.80

Trove Café and Bakery
WHITE SOURDOUGH

Our white sourdough is one of our most famous sourdough loaves. There are a number of cafés/restaurants across Manchester who have it on their menus. Below is the recipe. You can purchase the starter from our website and we will post it out to you. The final dough uses a little wholemeal flour along with the white flour, but if you don't have any, you can simply use 470g white flour instead.
Makes 1 loaf which is 800g.

Ingredients

440g white flour

30g wholemeal flour

10g salt

270ml water

180g levain

For the levain:

95ml water

85g flour

30g starter (fed and cared for levain, available from our website)

Method

Combine the ingredients in a bowl until all the flour is hydrated. Tip out onto the work surface and knead for 5 minutes. Add a little oil to the bowl and place the dough back in the bowl to prove in a warm place for 30-60 minutes. Check for fermentation – you're looking for bubbles and the smell of yoghurt or nuts!

After the proving time, remove the dough from the bowl and make folds into the middle of the dough. Shape it into a round boule (ball-like shape).

Preheat the oven to its maximum temperature.

Place the shaped loaf onto a baking tray, cover with a damp tea towel and allow to prove for 60-120 minutes in a warm place.

Slash and bake in the hot oven for 30-40 minutes. Place a oven proof bowl of water alongside the bread in the oven for extra crispy caramelisation!

The Best of
BRITISH

Traditions from Britain's past are kept alive in Manchester's historic chop houses, The Albert Square Chop House, Sam's Chop House and Mr Thomas's Chop House.

Housed in some of Manchester's finest buildings and celebrating the glorious heritage of hearty British dining, The Victorian Chop House Company is a local independent business that is founded on a shared love of British food, Victorian history and proud hospitality – a combination of values that makes their chop houses as popular today as they were in the nineteenth century.

At the heart of Manchester, The Albert Square Chop House sits within the listed walls of Thomas Worthington's iconic Memorial Hall. The once-upon-a-time Victorian warehouse is now a converted post-industrial space with charming original features setting off its open kitchen. Chef Jacques Hilton can see out over the restaurant as he leads his team in preparing classic British dishes. The glorious building also contains a unique space that is perfect for holding events – from weddings and parties to meetings and private dining.

For a little more Mancunian history, Sam's Chop House is the place to go. Famous faces aplenty have been regulars over its long history from 1872, including the likes of L.S. Lowry. Established by local businessman Samuel Studd, Sam's Chop House remains one of Manchester's most celebrated bars and restaurants, with a fine selection of drinks on offer and a truly traditional range of British food.

The Grade II listed building which is home to Mr Thomas's Chop House first opened in 1870. A much loved local Manchester institution, the cast-iron framed building and terracotta block displaying Art Nouveau motifs makes one of the loveliest settings to enjoy the very best British cuisine. From its fine beers and wines to its authentic British dishes cooked with modern twists, this is a restaurant that brings the best of the Victorian age to today's food lovers.

What unites these three thriving restaurants is their commitment to keeping historic British traditions alive, celebrating fine cooking and using the best local ingredients. There is also special attention to detail when it comes to the wines on offer, too. George Bergier, Head Sommelier hand-picks the wine lists for all three chop houses. Nobody is more committed to fine wines: "I think I was born with a corkscrew in one hand and a wine glass in the other."

The Albert Square Chop House
SEARED SCALLOPS

with slow-braised ox cheek and cauliflower

The ox cheek takes about 8 hours to cook to tender perfection. Serves 4.

Ingredients

100g Romanesque cauliflower florets (or standard cauliflower)

40g salted butter

12 scallops

Lemon wedge

Salt and pepper

For the slow-braised ox cheek:

1 small ox cheek (approx. 200g)

Beef stock (enough to cover, approximately 300ml)

1 sprig of thyme

1 sprig of rosemary

For the cauliflower purée:

40ml vegetable oil

400g cauliflower, cut into small florets

2 small shallots, peeled and finely diced

1 clove garlic, peeled and finely chopped

270ml whipping cream

60ml water

Method

For the ox cheek

Preheat the oven to 110°C. Place the ox cheek into an ovenproof dish and cover with stock so totally immersed. Add the thyme and rosemary and place in the oven and slow-cook for about 8 hours until tender. Remove the braised cheek from the stock and set aside. Remove the herb sprigs and strain the stock through a sieve into a small pan. Place the stock back on the heat at a low heat and reduce until the sauce is a glossy, coating consistency. Slice the cooked ox cheek into four pieces.

For the cauliflower purée

Add the oil to a small saucepan then sweat the cauliflower, shallot and garlic until slightly caramelised and golden brown. Add the cream, bring to the boil, then reduce to a simmer and cook for approximately 10 minutes until the cauliflower is soft. While still hot, remove from the heat and carefully purée in a food processor until smooth. Add a splash of water so you get the correct consistency, then season with salt and pepper to taste.

Cook the Romanesque cauliflower in salted boiling water until tender and al dente, then remove and finish with 20g melted butter, salt and pepper.

Place the sliced ox cheek back into the sauce to warm through. Warm the cauliflower purée in a small saucepan. Pan roast the scallops in a hot pan until golden brown and glazed, then finish with a squeeze of lemon, the remaining 20g butter and some salt and pepper. Arrange neatly on four warm plates and serve.

Mr Thomas
FAMOUS CORNED BEEF HASH

The secret to Tom's corned beef hash is in the long eight-day brining. Serves 4.

Ingredients

For the beef in brine:

3 litres water

180g salt

60g sugar

2 onions, peeled and halved

2 bay leaves

A pinch of black peppercorns

500g beef brisket

For the corned beef hash:

500ml beef stock

800g Maris Piper potatoes, peeled and diced into 2cm dice

30ml vegetable oil

400g onion, finely diced

1 clove garlic, peeled and finely chopped

1 tsp fresh rosemary, picked and chopped

1 tsp fresh thyme, picked and chopped

60g beef dripping

300ml gravy, heated

1 tbsp chives, finely chopped

4 poached eggs

4 rashers of bacon

Method

Make the brining liquor by combining the water, salt, sugar, onions, bay leaves and peppercorns in a large container. Place the beef brisket into the brining liquor so totally immersed and store in the fridge. Remove from the brine after 8 days and rinse thoroughly under running cold water for at least 30 minutes.

Preheat the oven to 110°C. Cut the brisket and place in large ovenproof roasting dish. Cover with beef stock then cover with foil. Slow-roast in the oven for approximately 6-8 hours until the meat is almost falling apart. Remove from the pan and allow to cool.

Meanwhile boil the diced potatoes until cooked, but still tender with bite. Drain. Roughly dice the beef, place in a bowl add the cooked potatoes. In a large frying pan, heat the vegetable oil and fry the diced onions, garlic, chopped rosemary and thyme. Allow to cool then add to the beef and potatoes.

Using the same frying pan, now fry the hash mixture in the beef dripping on a high heat until crispy and brown. When ready, stir in two-thirds of the heated gravy and chopped chives.

Spoon the hot hash into a ring in the centre of plate, then push down with the back of the spoon, repeat this for each portion. Garnish with a warm poached egg, crispy bacon rashers, a sprinkle of chopped chives and a drizzle of the remaining gravy. Accompany with the legendary HP sauce.

Sam's
RICE PUDDING

L.S. Lowry's favourite vanilla rice pudding with home-made mixed berry jam.
Serves 4.

Ingredients

For the mixed berry jam:

400g frozen mixed berries

150g caster sugar

For the rice pudding:

150g pudding rice

300ml double cream

100g caster sugar

700ml whole milk

1 vanilla pod

Method

For the jam, place a thick-bottomed pan onto the heat and allow to get very hot. Carefully add the frozen berries into the hot pan with the sugar. Stir and allow to boil, then continue stirring and turn down the heat. Remove from the heat and allow to cool.

For the rice pudding, place the pudding rice, cream, sugar and milk into a thick-bottomed saucepan. Split the vanilla pod lengthwise and extract the seeds with a tip of a knife. Add the seeds and scraped pod to the pan.

Bring all the ingredients to the boil, then reduce to a slow simmer on a low heat for approximately 30 minutes, until the rice is cooked and the mixture is thick and creamy.

Allow to stand for 5-10 minutes. Remove the vanilla pod and discard. Divide into four warm bowls and serve with the mixed berry jam.

Fine Dining with
RUSTIC CHARM

Overlooking Manchester and the Cheshire plain beyond from its enviable hill-top location on the edge of the Pennines, The White Hart describes itself as a village pub and a little more besides…

Although the team at The White Hart may fondly describe their pub as a Saddleworth village pub where the emphasis is on putting a smile on every customer's face, one glance at the string of accolades they've achieved and it's obvious that this is no ordinary local.

An AA 4-star rated inn with two AA rosettes for its food, a top-50 pub in the Waitrose Good Food Guide 2016 and listed in the Michelin guide, the stone-walled pub, hotel, restaurant and wedding venue doesn't shout about its myriad successes. Instead it focuses on making sure each individual guest leaves happy after every visit.

The multiple dining options include traditional and affordable classics in The Brasserie, from comforting fish pie or old English sausage with mash and gravy to fillet steak served with hand-cooked chips or grilled whole lemon sole with brown shrimp and almond butter. Each dish is cooked to perfection with love, skill and imagination.

The White Hart also offers The Dining Room, with a highly celebrated menu and cocktail list. The dazzling dishes are created with flair and imagination using the very best ingredients from around the globe. Think sashimi tuna with pickled mushrooms, soya emulsion and black radish; scallop carpaccio with cauliflower caviar, horseradish and mustard leaf; or squab pigeon, variations of onion and goat's curd – and that's just for starters. With main courses including butter-poached halibut, roast partridge and Gressingham duck, there is no question that this is fine dining to be savoured.

The Head Chef, Michael Shaw, is the embodiment of what makes the food here so special. He was brought up just a stone's throw from The White Hart, started his career at Le Manoir aux Quat'Saisons under the illustrious Raymond Blanc and has since developed his culinary career working under Richard Neat in France and Marco Pierre White in London before moving back to the north of England where he was Head Chef at Gilpin Lodge when it gained its first Michelin star.

Twelve deluxe en-suite rooms are situated in the original building, which dates back to 1788 and weddings, conferences and events are popular in the various spaces of this stunningly appointed venue. Whatever the occasion, The White Hart ticks all the boxes – whether it's for its food, wine, rooms or dedicated service.

Photos: www.bacononthebeech.com

The White Hart
RHUBARB SOUFFLE, GINGER ICE CREAM

One of the impressive desserts from The Dining Room, this is a
stunning combination of flavours. Serves 4.

Ingredients

Soufflé base

350g rhubarb purée

100g caster sugar

18g cornflour

For the soufflé pots

50g soft butter

25g caster sugar

For the meringue

3 egg whites

60g sugar

Ginger ice cream

320ml double cream

280ml milk

100g root ginger

7 egg yolks

165g caster sugar

Method

Dissolve the sugar in just enough water and cook until it reaches 114°C, Remove from
the heat and whisk in rhubarb puree, return back to the heat and bring to the boil. Dilute
the cornflour with a little water and pour into the rhubarb purée. Whisk until you see one
bubble and remove from the heat, leave to cool then pass through a fine sieve.

Brush soufflé pots with soft butter, add sugar and spin the pot around until butter is evenly
coated.

Whisk the egg whites until lightly whipped, then add sugar and whisk until soft peak, put
3 tablespoons of the rhubarb base into a bowl and lightly fold in soft peaked egg white,
fill soufflé pots to the top, using a palate knife scrap the top of the soufflé pot so it is flat.
Cook soufflés at 190°C for about 8 minutes.

Place the cream and milk in a saucepan, peel and roughly chop the ginger. Add to the pan
and bring to the boil. Leave to infuse for about 6 hours then reboil the cream mixture,
whisk the yolks and sugar until you get thick ribbons. Pour cream the mixture onto yolks
and stir until well blended, cook in a bowl over simmering water, stirring, until the custard
covers the back of a spoon. Do not boil or eggs will scramble, strain through a sieve and
leave to cool. Churn in 2 batches for about 20 minutes.

More Than A CURRY

Health, vitality, fun and passion are at the centre of the award-winning Indian and Pakistani restaurant Zouk Tea Bar and Grill.

The two brothers behind the success of Zouk Tea Bar and Grill are, in some respects, as different as chalk and cheese – Tayub, the Managing Director, with his calm, focused business brain and Mudassar, the Creative Director, with his energetic passion for all things food – yet this committed pair share an infectious enthusiasm for innovation, cooking and supporting the community.

Tayub and Mudassar grew up in a food-loving family. They both worked in their father's restaurant before going to university. They soon both decided the corporate world wasn't for them and found themselves drawn back to the irresistible world of food. They wanted to open a restaurant that moved away from what the British public expected from an Indian restaurant; to develop a new generation of restaurant based around their shared values of health, vitality, fun and passion.

Tayub's strategic thinking and eye for detail combined with Mudassar's passion for seeking out new flavours and techniques allowed them to create a modern restaurant that became an instant hit. Innovative cooking takes place in the theatre-style kitchen, which runs the full length of the

restaurant, adding to the captivating atmosphere. Diners are fascinated to see their dishes being skilfully cooked before their eyes, dispelling those out-dated ideas that Indian food in the UK relies on pre-prepared sauces.

Seafood is a big hit with the regulars who adore the spiced calamari and spicy prawn cakes, which are made with the freshest and best ingredients available each day. The grill menu is extensive, showcasing the variety of food available within the modern Indian and Pakistani culinary cultures – it's certainly not just curry here!

A host of awards has been received by this dynamic duo in recognition of their endless commitment to top-quality dining – in fact, they were voted Best Restaurant by the Manchester Tourism Awards in 2012 and recently were awarded North West Winner at the 2015 Best in Britain (BIBA) awards organised as part of National Curry Week. With continued investment back into the business as well as into the local community, the future is looking incredibly bright for this much-loved Manchester restaurant.

Zouk Tea Bar
CHICKEN HALEEM

Haleem is traditionally made with lamb or sometimes with beef and originates from Pakistan. It is a delicious slow-cooked stew recipe that has wonderful flavours. This version uses chicken in place of the red meat to offer a slightly healthier alternative. It also traditionally includes cracked wheat which helps give it a thick soupy consistency and we do use this in our restaurant version, but this recipe has omitted this so its suitable for anybody with a wheat intolerance too. Haleem is the perfect meal for a cold wintery day – it is like having a warming chicken stew or thick soup and it is packed full of goodness and flavour. Serves 4.

Ingredients

300g haleem mixed lentils *

500ml water

2 large chicken breasts

4 tbsp vegetable oil or ghee

1 onion, diced

2-3 green chillies, sliced (depending on how much spice you would like)

3 tbsp haleem masala (you can find this in packets in Asian supermarkets)

2 tsp salt

1 tbsp lemon juice

To serve:

Lemon wedges

Fresh coriander

Sliced fresh green chilli

Garam masala

Fresh ginger

Fried onions (finely sliced and fried in 1 tbsp vegetable oil)

Method

Rinse the lentils. Bring the water to the boil in a pan, add the lentils, bring back to the boil and simmer for 30 minutes. Reserve the cooking water.

Coarsely dice the chicken breasts and add to a separate pan. Cover with boiling water and boil until cooked through – this should take about 15-20 minutes. Drain and put to one side.

Heat the oil or ghee in a saucepan and gently fry the onion for about 5 minutes until browned and starting to caramelise. Add the green chillies and fry for 1 minute further. Add the chicken, haleem masala, lentils, salt and lemon juice to the onions and chilli mixture, then add the reserved cooking water from the lentils and stir well.

Take a hand blender and very lightly blitz the mixture to shred the chicken. You don't want to turn it to mush you just want the chicken to shred into slivers, so only pulse very lightly. Return the pan to the heat and cook for 10 minutes further.

While the haleem is cooking through prepare the garnishes.

Put the haleem in a serving dish or dishes and sprinkle with the fried onions. Then serve. Haleem can be served with rice or bread – it is best with a roti or naan to mop up the juices. It must also be served with an array of spices and garnishes as the idea is to tailor it to your tastes. Place all the garnishes on a saucer or in small ramekins if you have them and bring out to the table to everybody can help themselves.

*You can find these in Asian supermarkets, sometimes called broth mix. Also you may find it in your usual supermarket in the lentils and pulses section, named mixed lentils or again broth or soup mix. Generally it contains a fairly even mixture of pearl barley, red lentils, yellow split peas, green split peas and marrow fat peas. If you do wish to try making it with the cracked wheat, then add about 50g to the lentils half way through their cooking time.

The science OF BREWING

Inspired by nature, science and cultural history, Zymurgorium is Manchester's first distillery and the UK's first craft meadery.

The intriguing name Zymurgorium is a delicious mix of two words that reflects founder Aaron Darke's love of experimentation and creating new things. "Zymurgy" is the practice of fermentation in brewing and distilling, and "emporium" is a store selling a variety of things – put these together and you get a wonderful shop of varied brews!

Aaron has always been fascinated by science and nature, two things which can seem at complete opposite ends of our cultural spectrum, yet are so intrinsically linked. He studied science at university, and while his academic time was spent learning in the classroom, he spent his spare time brewing for his friends. Never one to use shop-bought kits, he would forage for ingredients and work out his own brewing processes, putting his scientific studies to use in the biology, chemistry and physics involved and his tastebuds to use in experimenting with flavour combinations.

By the end of his degree it was clear to him that he loved brewing more than anything in the lab, and he began work on his business, which became Zymurgorium in 2013. It all began with mead, which is quite fitting since it is one of the world's oldest alcoholic drinks. Aaron, with support from his brother Callum, saw the potential in this ancient brew – so interesting and diverse – and the brothers set about creating a new breed of the drink that would entice today's discerning drinkers.

Zymurgorium became the UK's first craft meadery. Aaron, along with this brother, experiments with various honeys, grows his own ingredients and forages for new and unusual things to try in his mead. He sees endless opportunity in the natural world for new flavours and the discoveries are leading to his ever-expanding emporium of modern meads.

Mead might be where it all started, but it's the tip of the iceberg for these ambitious brewers. Ciders, beers and spirits are also being created in his Manchester brewery, and they can also add the title of Manchester's first distillery to the list of achievements! The Manchester original gin and vodka are certainly causing a buzz among the local cocktail-makers, and with flavour infusions like pink grapefruit gin and very fine toffee vodka, it's easy to see why. One thing we can be sure of – there will be plenty more exciting products coming our way in the future.

Zyurgorium
STRATASPHERIC AVIATOR

1 part refers to a 25ml shot for these recipes, but you can scale them up if
serving to more people. Serves 1.

Ingredients

*1 part Zyurgorium Original
Manchester Gin*

2 parts Zymurgorium Violet Gin

1 part clear kirsch liqueur

Crushed ice

*3 glazed cherries on a cocktail stick,
to garnish*

Method

Shake both types of gin and the kirsch in a cocktail shaker and serve in a martini glass
with crushed ice (ideally) and the cocktail cherry garnish.

Zyurgorium
CRANACHAN

1 part refers to a 25ml shot for these recipes, but you can scale them up if
serving to more people. Serves 1.

Ingredients

*2 parts Zymurgorium Superior
Sweet Mead*

1 part smooth Scotch (non-peated)

*1 part Zymurgorium Raspberry
Liqueur*

Honey

Ice (optional)

Method

Lace the rim of a pre-chilled martini glass or Glencairn glass with honey. Alternatively,
lace the rim of the glass and add some ice. Add the mead, Scotch and raspberry liqueur
and stir.

The DIRECTORY

These great businesses have supported the making of this book; please support and enjoy them.

63 Degrees
104 High Street, Northern Quarter
Manchester M4 1HQ
Telephone: 0161 832 5438
Website: www.63degrees.co.uk
Twitter: @63DegreesNQ
French cooking to delight the senses using the finest fresh ingredients.

Abel Heywood
38 Turner Street, Northern Quarter
Manchester M4 1DZ
Telephone: 0161 819 1441
Website:
www.abelheywood.co.uk
Email:
abelheywood@hydesbrewery.com
Award-winning pub, restaurant and boutique hotel with 15 stunning rooms.

Albert's Restaurant and Bar
Quality food at a reasonable price in a sharp, modern space with friendly, unpretentious service.

Albert's Shed
20 Castle Street
Manchester M3 4LZ
Telephone: 0161 839 9818
Website: www.albertsshed.com

Albert's Didsbury
120-122 Barlow Moor Rd, West Didsbury
Manchester M20 2PU
Telephone: 0161 434 8289
Website: www. albertsdidsbury.com

Albert's Worsley
East Lancashire Road
Manchester M27 0AA
Telephone: 0161 794 1234
Website: www.albertsworsley.com

And the Dish Ran Away with the Spoon
230 Burton Road, West Didsbury
Manchester M20 2LW
Telephone: 0161 637 5517
Website:
www. dishandspoonfood.co.uk
Email:
thebaker@dishandspoonfood.co.uk
Café and tea room serving the finest teas, coffees and home-made cakes.

Bisous Bisous
663 Wilmslow Road, Didsbury
Manchester M20 6RA
Telephone: 0161 222 4480
Website: www.bisousbisous.co.uk
Twitter: @_bisousbisous
Authentic French pâtisserie in the heart of Didsbury.

Bollywood Masala
15-25 Liverpool Road
Manchester
M3 4NW
Telephone: 0161 839 3432
Website: www.bollywoodmasalauk.com
Award-winning Indian restaurant featuring modern flavours from around the world.

Brassica Grill
27 Shaw Road, Heaton Moor
Manchester SK4 4AG
Telephone: 0161 442 6730
Website: www.brassicagrill.com
Facebook:
www.facebook.com/brassicagrill
Twitter: @brassicagrill
Succulent steaks and grills to modern British cuisine, using locally sourced and seasonal ingredients.

Butcher's Quarter
66 Tib Street, Northern Quarter
Manchester M4 1LG
Telephone: 0161 637 9700
Website: www.butchers-quarter.co.uk
Email: info@butchers-quarter.co.uk
Facebook:
facebook.com/butchersquarter
Twitter: @butchersquarter
Butcher in Manchester's trendy Northern Quarter, selling local free-range meat, eggs, charcuterie, cheese and wines.

Bury Black Pudding Company
Units 12-14, J2 Business Park
Bridgehall Lane
Bury BL9 7NY
Telephone: 0161 797 0689
Website:
www.buryblackpuddings.co.uk
The finest award-winning black puddings made in Bury.

Croma
Website: www.cromapizza.co.uk
Independent Gourmet Pizzeria (Est 2000)

Manchester
1-3 Clarence St, Albert Square
Manchester M2 4DE
Telephone: 0161 237 9799

Chorlton
500 Wilbraham Road, Chorlton
Manchester M21 9AP
Telephone: 0161 881 1117

Prestwich
30 Longfield Centre, Prestwich
Manchester M25 1AY
Telephone: 0161 798 7666

Didsbury
651a Wilmslow Road, Didsbury
Manchester M20 6QZ
Telephone: 0161 445 6944

Dormouse Chocolates
Website:
www.dormousechocolates.co.uk
Twitter: @Dormousechocs
Manchester's first bean-to-bar chocolatier, making hand-made truffles and bars.

Epicerie Ludo
46 Beech Road, Chorlton-Cum-Hardy
Manchester M21 9EG
Telephone: 0161 861 0861
Website: www.epicerieludo.co.uk
Award-winning independent deli, wine merchant and fine grocery store.

George Charles
246 Burton Road, West Didsbury
Manchester M20 2LW
Telephone: 0161 445 4999
Facebook:
www.facebook.com/
GeorgeCharlesDidsbury
Twitter: @DidsburyGeorge
Newly established pub with a range of local and international beers and home-cooked food.

Harvey Nichols Brasserie and Bar
21 New Cathedral Street
Manchester M1 1AD
Telephone: 0161 828 8898
Website:
www.harveynichols.com/restaurant/
manchester-dining
The Second Floor Brasserie offers a relaxed yet stylish environment in which to enjoy all-day dining.

Ibérica
The Avenue, 3 Hardman Street,
Spinningfields
Manchester M3 3HF
Telephone: 0161 358 1350
Website: www.ibericarestaurants.com
Ibérica brings the very best in Spanish gastronomy, wine and culture to Manchester.

Lime
The Lowry Outlet Mall
Salford Quays M50 3AG
Telephone: 0161 869 0440
Website: www.limeuk.com
Independent restaurant and bar situated at the heart of Salford Quays.

Manchester House
18-22 Bridge Street, Spinningfields
Manchester M3 3BZ
Telephone: 0161 835 2557
Website:
www.manchesterhouse.uk.com
Twitter: @MCRHouse
Award-winning fine-dining restaurant and lounge bar.

The Manchester Tart Company
Telephone: 07810 423 190
Website: www.
themanchestertartcompany.co.uk
Email: info@
themanchestertartcompany.co.uk
Twitter: @mcrtarts
Award-winning range of hand-made pies and tarts, using regional recipes and locally produced seasonal ingredients.

Mark Andrew Developments
www.markandrewdevelopments.com
Landmarks of Manchester's Social Scene

Infamous Diner
3-5 Basil Chambers, Nicholas Croft
Manchester M4 1EY
Telephone: 0161 819 1798
Website: www.infamousdiner.co.uk
Twitter: @InfamousDiner

Rosylee
11 Stevenson Sq, Northern Quarter
Manchester M1 1DB
Telephone: 0161 228 6629
Website: www.rosylee.com
Twitter: @rosyleemcr

The Fitzgerald
11 Stevenson Sq, Northern Quarter
Manchester M1 1DB
Website: ww.thefitzgeraldnq.co.uk
Twitter: @TheFitzgeraldNQ

Walrus
78-88 High Street, Norther Quarter
Manchester M4 1ES
Website: www.walrusmanchester.com
Twitter: @WalrusMCR

The Metropolitan
2 Lapwing Lane, West Didsbury
Manchester M20 2WS
Telephone: 0161 438 2332
Website: www.the-metropolitan.co.uk
Fine real ales, continental beers, malt whiskies and fine wines to complement the excellent food.

Mish Mash
133 Beech Road, Chorlton-cum-Hardy
Manchester M21 9EQ
Telephone: 0161 862 0485
Website: www.mishmashbars.com
Facebook: www.facebook.com/mishmashbar
Twitter: @mishmashbar
Classic British cooking, global flavours and local produce combined in a fresh, funky, interesting and delicious menu.

Mr Cooper's House & Garden
The Midland Hotel, Peter Street
Manchester M60 2DS
Telephone: 0161 932 4198
Website: www.mrcoopershouseandgarden.co.uk
Email: info@mrcoopershouseandgarden.co.uk
Twitter: @mrcoopershouse
Brasserie-style cooking from Simon Rogan served in unique surroundings within the Midland Hotel.

Palate
516 Wilbraham Road, Chorlton-Cum-Hardy
Manchester M21 9AW
Telephone: 0161 882 0286
Website: www.palatechorlton.co.uk
Modern wine bar and restaurant serving small plates, main dishes and British cheese and charcuterie.

Podium, Hilton Manchester Deansgate
303 Deansgate
Manchester M3 4LQ
Telephone: 0161 870 1600
Website: www.manchesterdeansgate.hilton.com
Informal and intimate, the restaurant offers a casual dining experience with locally sourced ingredients to create cuisine that is both international and modern.

Pokusevski's
13 Shaw Road, Heaton Moor
Stockport SK4 4AG
Telephone: 0161 442 1717
and
Bridge House, Media City UK
Salford Quays M50 2BH
Telephone: 0161 713 3749
Website: www.pokusevski.com
Email: info@pokusevskis.com
Facebook: facebook.com/pokusevskis
Twitter: @pokusevskis
Great tasting, home-cooked food in relaxed and informal surroundings.

Salvi's
Website: www.salvismanchester.co.uk
Twitter: @SalvisMcr
An independent, family-run delicatessen and eatery.
Salvi's Mozzarella Bar
Unit 22b The Corn Exchange
Manchester M4 3TR
Telephone: 0161 222 8021
Salvi's Cucina and Salvi's Rosticceria
19 John Dalton Street
Manchester M2 6FW
Telephone: 0161 222 8090

Slice Pizza & Bread Bar
1a Stevenson Square, Northern Quarter
Manchester M1 1DN
Telephone: 0161 236 9032
Website: www.slicepizza.co
Authentic pizza baked with passion, served by the slice.

Tampopo
Website: www.tampopo.co.uk
Twitter: @TampopoEats
Fresh Eastern cooking inspired by authentic street food.

Tampopo Albert Square
16 Albert Square,
Manchester M2 5PF
Telephone: 0161 819 1966

Tampopo Corn Exchange
Corn Exchange
Manchester M4 3TR
Telephone: 0161 839 6484

Tampopo Trafford Centre
The Orient, Trafford Centre
Manchester M17 8EH
Telephone: 0161 747 8878

Teacup Kitchen
55 Thomas Street
Manchester M4 1NA
Telephone: 0161 832 3233
Website: www. teacupandcakes.com
Quirky Northern Quarter café serving loose-leaf teas, cakes, breakfasts, lunches and afternoon tea.

The Parlour
60 Beech Road, Chorlton
Manchester M21 9EG
Telephone: 0161 881 4871
Website: www.theparlour.info
The character and spirit of a traditional British pub with a modern, grown-up edge.

The Rose Garden
218 Burton Road, West Didsbury
Manchester M20 2LW
Telephone: 0161 478 0747
Website:
www.therosegardendidsbury.com
Award-winning contemporary restaurant serving modern British cuisine.

The Albert Square Chop House
The Memorial Hall, Albert Square
Manchester M2 5PF
Telephone: 0161 834 1866
Website:
www.albertsquarechophouse.com
Dining pub and British restaurant in the iconic Memorial Hall.

Sam's Chop House
Back Pool Fold off Cross Street
Manchester M2 1HN
Telephone: 0161 834 3210
Website: www.samschophouse.com
The best British cuisine and a fine selection of ales, wines and spirits.

Mr Thomas's Chop House
52 Cross Street
Manchester M2 7AR
Telephone: 0161 832 2245
Website: www.tomschophouse.com
Fine food, fine wines, good beer and great company.

The White Hart
51 Stockport Road, Lydgate
Oldham OL4 4JJ
Telephone: 01457 872566
Website: www.thewhitehart.co.uk
AA 4-star rated inn and Michelin-listed restaurant with various dining options.

Trove café and bakery
1032 Stockport Rd, Levenshulme
Manchester M19 3WX
Café: 0161 2248588
Bakery: 0161 4327184
Website: www.trovefoods.co.uk
Café serving seasonal hand-made food and bakery producing artisan bread.

Zouk Tea Bar and Grill
Unit 5, The Quadrangle, Chester Street
Manchester M1 5QS
Telephone: 0161 233 1090
Website: www.zoukteabar.co.uk
New generation Indian and Pakistani restaurant in the heart of the city.

Zymurgorium
Unit 19 Irlam Business Centre
Soapstone way, Irlam
Manchester M44 6RA
Website: www.zymurgorium.com
Email: Info@zymurgorium.com
The brewing emporium: an artisan distillery, meadery, cidery and brewery.

me:ze
PUBLISHING

Other titles in this series

The Sheffield Cook Book features Baldwin's Omega, Nonna's, Ashoka, Cubana, Peppercorn.
978-0-9928981-0-6

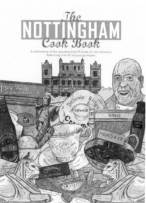

The Nottingham Cook Book features Sat Bains with Rooms, World Service, Harts, Escabeche
978-0-9928981-5-1

The Derbyshire Cook Book features Chatsworth Estate, Fischers of Baslow, Thornbridge Brewery
978-0-9928981-7-5

The Suffolk Cook Book featuring Jimmys Farm, Gressingham Duck etc.
978-1-910863-02-2

The Cambridgeshire Cook Book features Midsummer House, The Pint Shop, Gog Magog Hills, Clare College
978-0-9928981-9-9

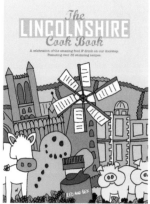

The Lincolnshire Cook Book featuring Colin Mcgurran, TV Chef Rachel Green & San Pietro etc.
978-1-910863-05-3

All available from Waterstones, Amazon, independent bookshops and all establishments featured in the book.

FIND OUT MORE ABOUT MEZE PUBLISHING AT WWW.MEZEPUBLISHING.CO.UK